MAKE M

MONEY FROM

PROPERTY

FROM INVESTOR THINKING TO A BUSINESS MINDSET

SECOND EDITION

— VICKI WUSCHE —

Make More Money from Property:
From investor thinking to a business mindset
2nd Edition
Copyright ©2017 Vicki Wusche

First edition published in 2012 by SRA Books
Second edition published in 2017 by SRA Books
suerichardson.co.uk

ISBN 978-1-909116-96-2
eISBN 978-1-909116-97-9

A CIP record for this book is available from the British Library.

Printed in the United Kingdom.

Make More Money from Property: From investor thinking to a business mindset is honest and truthful about what it takes to be a success in your finances. Vicki understands that it takes more than just information; it also requires a knowledge of how to implement the actions that will bring success. Highly recommended.

Denzil Edmeade
www.gen-hope.co.uk

Make More Money from Property encourages you to examine your strategies, your portfolio and, most importantly, yourself. Vicki encourages the strategic development of your business – working on it not in it – alongside a solid life philosophy and core values. Happy investing!

Francis Dolley
www.yourlocalinvestment.com

I would recommend this book full of gems to even the most experienced investor.

Clare Gillbanks
www.the-property-angel.co.uk

We were mesmerised by the impactful clarity and depth. A gift of time, money and advanced knowledge from the best exponent of expertise that mere mortals can emulate.

Steve and Helen Green

It is an essential read for investors of all types and those who would like to play but don't know where or how to start.

Tom Evans, author of
Flavours of Thought

When it comes to property, Vicki simply knows her stuff! If you want someone who is going to tell you what it really takes to get out there and *Make Money from Property*, who is actually doing it and has hands on experience and a wealth of knowledge, then Vicki is the real deal.

Johnnie Cass
www.johnniecass.com

From the outset, the reader is encouraged to take active responsibility for achieving the wealth obtainable through property, to focus on the opportunities available and apply fresh thinking. *Make More Money from Property* comes highly recommended.

Lorraine Stylianou
www.frida-kahlo.co.uk

If your focus is to create a property sourcing business to enable you to generate cashflow and eventually save capital to invest in a portfolio for yourself, then this is the book for you. This book has really helped shape the way I have approached my property business. There is clear advice and a step-by-step approach. It is easy to read and easy to follow.

Lila Hall

Whether you have a portfolio or you are starting out – this book has great advice. This second edition is focused on providing you with a clear understanding of the business marketplace and the current financial environment. It encourages you to be clear on your goal and to set your expectations. The final section of the book offers a step-by-step explanation of how you can make more money from property more easily. Understand your business model now and get to work!

Bella King
www.bellakingdesign.co.uk

Contents

This book is dedicated to my family and friends –
those newly joined, those sadly departed. May
we all have the time to fulfill our dreams.

I love you.

Foreword

Vicki and I recently connected through our mutual interest in all things investment. Like me, Vicki believes that trying to get rich by trading Forex or stocks is like trying to win the lottery. Or worse. Like her, I believe that property investment is a great business opportunity.

This is the second edition of her book, newly reworked with additional case studies to prepare you, the new and experienced property investor, for the challenges that Brexit may bring, not only to property investment but to the wider economy. It's Vicki's commitment to helping others to take more control over their financial futures and her desire to educate on the difference between get rich quick and create wealth for the long term that is so refreshing.

This book focuses on sharing the practical tips you need to take to move from investor thinking to a clear business mindset. I like the fact that Vicki has taken the time to explain how important your mindset is and that taking responsibility for your financial future is crucial. Section two explains some of the background to lending and the wider economy without becoming too boring that you skip over the section!

Vicki seeks to raise your awareness of the importance of not just buying investment properties but also developing a business around long-term wealth creation and financial security. Drawing on her own experience of investing, and now as a business mentor, she explains practical tools that you can apply to your own personal finances, existing property strategy and your family's financial future.

If you are determined to be successful, then read on... Read again... And, above all, take action.

Robert Rolih
International bestselling author of *The Million Dollar Decision*

Acknowledgements

One day, I will write a book of gratitude and list all the wonderful people I have been so blessed to meet and to have been supported by.

I will mention just one here. There are many more, you know who you are, and please know that I am eternally grateful.

Sue Richardson, my publisher, without whose help none of this would have been possible. Her insights into the business, strategy, marketing and world of books have helped me to raise the standard of this book to new heights.

And, of course, boundless gratitude to my family; especially my beautiful and brilliant daughters, Kimberley and Charlie, and our new granddaughter Amelia – the start of another new generation. Last, but not least, my darling and much loved Bob. My tireless supporter, the man with the most patience in the world – 'everyone needs a Bob' – I love you so much.

I love you all so much, thank you!

INTRODUCTION

Training and education versus
understanding; information
versus knowledge

Introduction

Training and education versus understanding; information versus knowledge

£1,000s and £1,000s – are you getting a return?

If property training companies are training thousands of people on how to invest in property – the theory and techniques of how to invest in property – then why are so few people actually taking action and buying property? Also, why are so few people seeing a return on the thousands of pounds that they are spending to get this information?

It is because there is a difference between information and knowledge; a difference between training and understanding. If we really accepted the best financial information available, why did we suffer such a massive financial crisis?

Information, like training and education, is what you receive when you go to school. Teachers teach you – in theory – out of context. Please do not misunderstand me; I am not disregarding all property training courses. There are some good courses and there are numerous people who will achieve success, regardless of the teacher or teaching techniques. Knowledge and understanding comes from experience – current real-world experience – contextualised, because you are living in the moment.

When I first studied property investment in 2008, I learnt from people experienced in investing. None of us had ever experienced the disastrous recession that was about to befall us. Therefore, everything I learnt was historic, static and not in preparation for the economic and now political changes to come. This theoretical learning out of context, causes the learner to misunderstand and fail to adapt when sudden shifts in the marketplace occur. Since this book was first published, we have seen seismic shifts and there are still more to come.

The same is true of so many people once they leave a property training course. They have learnt a variety of strategies in a theoretical context. They do not know and understand the 'geo-political-economic' landscape that today's successful and professional property investors are competing in. Buy the right property and they will have cashflow; buy the wrong property and they will suffer financially. This is because they have been trained, they have information, but they don't yet have the knowledge and understanding that comes with experience.

What is happening in our world? This is a coming of a new order, a new age. Not just a transition from the agricultural age to the industrial age to the information age. This is different. This is about different ways of thinking on a global scale in a world that is so interconnected that what happens in Japan, Africa or America is as relevant to your personal household as if your neighbours played loud music through the walls or parked across your drive.

Being trained by people who are not currently buying in today's real world economy is a recipe for disaster. I would go further and state that listening only to people who started their portfolios in a time of boom, plentiful lending and remortgaging strategies that led to many people having zero equity in a portfolio is also a poor recipe.

The economy is 'doomed'

The world economy, our country and possibly even some individuals are 'doomed'. Why? Because everything is interconnected:

- An American president builds a wall and changes the trading relations of countries across the world, somewhere your tenant loses their job and your rent does not get paid; or...

- One Eurocrat demands punitive punishments as we seek to regain balance and funding in your region suddenly shifted – a disaster; or...

- Government attitude towards the private landlord shifts, combined with rigorous lending criteria and tax demands – do you stop investing and sell up...?

Is this the future you want?

Do you just have information and strategies or do you have the knowledge and understanding to make the right decisions in a dynamic, exciting and volatile economic environment? Are you learning from people who started to build their wealth in these uncertain times – were they like you with little or no savings?

This is such an exciting time. Millionaires are created in times like this. Those who know how to use other people's money to leverage, and take action on that knowledge, will create significant investment portfolios that will provide for them and their families for generations to come. (See Vicki Wusche, *Using Other People's Money: How to Invest in Property*, 2016.)

Those prepared to let go of outdated information and beliefs and let a new body of knowledge and understanding take its place will be able to lie back and enjoy life.

Are you prepared to think differently about how you can create wealth, financial security and financial stability?

The aim of this book is to help you leverage your knowledge, and to leverage my knowledge and understanding. It is to help you develop your financial and business education and become a successful professional property investor and business owner.

The future is not about 'me first and stuff you'; it's going to be about 'we can do it – I am doing it – come on, join me and take action'. Take active responsibility for *your* life, *your* future, *your* wealth and income.

Do you want to make more money from your property knowledge?

I was taught three crucial lessons about property:

1.   Buy at discount.
2.   Circulate your money.
3.   Cashflow, cashflow, cashflow!

While I do believe in these three fundamental rules, I also believe that I was misled.

In my experience, the detail lying behind these headline rules is costing you money, and lots of it!

- Have you spent money on property training (maybe, like me, as much as £10,000–£20,000)?
- Have you still not seen a return on that investment?
- How many potential deals are you wasting because they don't fit the criteria you were taught?

For me, this really came to a head when someone contacted me through Facebook and asked me to send them the details of all of my deals over the last 6–12 months for analysis. They said that they had not been able to find any deals where they could get all of their money back within six months. I am not surprised! House prices and lending rules are just a few of the hurdles to be negotiated.

I have only been able to get all of my money back out of a deal within months on four out of over 70 properties bought for myself and bespoke clients. I achieved it on those four specifically because I negotiated a commercial funding deal with my bank to enable me to replicate the old 'Mortgage Express' style of buying for cash and then remortgaging. More importantly, what deals were being missed in pursuit of the goose that laid the golden egg?

The aim of this book is to share what I have learnt about property investing over the last three years so that you can:

- learn the truth about investing in this new and constantly evolving economic market
- leverage your knowledge, skills, experience and passion to develop a phenomenal cashflowing property investing business
- be living the life of your dreams within 18 months.

Unlike many people in the market today, I don't have a massive property portfolio that I could remortgage and release capital to buy property. When starting out, I was not prepared to commit mortgage fraud and lie to lenders so that I could own a property with no equity and poor cashflow. I started with a pot of £80,000 contributed by family members. I turned this into our first five properties that generated an average net cashflow of £1,000 per month. This was a massive 15% return on investment (ROI) – you definitely can't achieve this today via the banks or stock market. Even allowing 25% for disasters, voids and repairs, the investment would still return 11.25%.

What I have discovered is that building a successful property business requires three things:

1. A business mindset.
2. An understanding of the economic environment.
3. Knowledge on how to turn the theory into an active and personal cashflowing strategy.

Are you ready to step up your game?

This book is designed to give you a head start at creating your own cashflowing property business. In my business, I focus on property sourcing as a business model. This enables me to focus on buying fantastic cashflowing investment properties for myself and, when my cash is busy, I turn to buying for my bespoke clients. They, in turn, pay me for my knowledge, experience and skill, which provides me with more cash to invest back into property.

Throughout the chapters of this book, I will often make reference to the fact that these are new and unpredictable times, both economically and politically as we face the challenge of Brexit and beyond. It is vital that you consider this in all that you read, both in this book and others. In addition, it is vital that you consider this in every decision that you make both now and in the future. Why? Because how someone built their portfolio in 2005, 2010 or even 2015 bears no relation to how you can start or grow your portfolio now. The easy lending criteria pre-2015 is dead; there are now more taxes and new challenges. We still need to invest and circulate our money, of course, but not to the detriment of cashflow, equity, good deals and common sense.

We have moved from a period of 'mad investing' (where over-valued properties were over leveraged with 100% funding and now fail to provide significant cashflow) to a second potential period of 'bad investing' where, as the availability of funds start to shrink, some investors will become increasingly 'creative' and discover new ways to deceive and circumvent the lending requirements and rules. This will lead to over-leveraged properties that risk negative equity and even zero cashflow all over again.

I started my property investing business in June 2008, though I will admit I did not recognise it as a business then. I completed on my first independently sourced property in August 2008. Over the following four months, I faced more challenges than I could ever have thought imaginable and learnt more than I thought possible. I will cover many of those insights as we progress through the book.

It is crucial to note that when times (and lending) get tough, we need to be more determined to be successful. I, too, became creative in my financing strategies during 2009. However, instead of wandering into the grey areas of mortgage fraud and deception to trick the lenders, I looked for other ways to continue investing. I learnt how to use other people's money to invest in property (see my first book, *Using Other People's Money*).

This book moves on from the specific strategies that I explored and used during that time to explain the business critical skills that are transferable to any business model you choose. The skills that I gained have enabled me to grow my sourcing business into a bespoke high-value service. I have also developed a property training business to share my knowledge and experience more widely, and help investors like you to reach financial freedom as easily and pain-free as possible. I remember speaking at a property event in 2010 and saying that 'I didn't want to create a business…'. I was wrong and misguided. Building a business is crucial to succeeding (even surviving) the next 5–7 years and building long-term financial security.

So, whether you are new to investing or experienced, this book is packed full of ideas and practical steps to help you turn your property knowledge into a business that can give you the 'lifestyle, cashflowing dream-machine' you wish for – all you have to do is work hard.

'Fortunately, there are many ways to financial heaven. I have found my way… It is up to you to find your way. This book is merely a guide, not an answer book, because in the real world there are no right answers… Only answers that work for you.'

Robert Kiyosaki – *An Unfair Advantage: The Power of Financial Education*, 2011, p20

'Being a leader means doing things on your terms. Being a loser means not getting people to follow you.'

Tony Robbins – NAC, June 2011

'Any business has to make money… they get lost in turnover, spreadsheets, and the future… they need money this week!'

Lord Alan Sugar – NAC, June 2011

'The cause of any [business] failure is a defocusing from the most important thing – are we making any money?'

Lord Alan Sugar – NAC, June 2011

'Why hope when you can learn, understand, take action, achieve results and get stronger? I am not a helper. I am a teacher, a tough teacher that some won't be able to handle. I don't mince words, I rock most boats, I profess action, and I demand hard work today for freedom and happiness tomorrow.

…I know some people won't step up. They are simply too lazy, too scared, too comfortable or are basking in the lull of false security to take charge of their lives. Some will come around. And when they do, I'll be there... I have many doors and every one of them is open to the willing, no matter their standing in life. Taking control all starts with a dream.'

Rich Dad – mission statement read at the start of each
game of CASHFLOW, Robert Kiyosaki

SECTION 1

The power of the mind – success
or failure, the choice is yours

Chapter 1

_____

Active responsibility – a new way of living

This chapter explains how you can take charge and create your future. It acts as an introduction to this radical new way of thinking about property investment. I will walk you through changes in understanding that you will immediately recognise as sensible and obvious, so obvious that you will adopt them with ease. Not in a dreamy unrealistic, intangible way, but by taking *active responsibility* for your financial future.

I will explain what responsibility will mean in your life – and how it will empower you to create your future. I will show you how leverage is the most powerful tool we can use as professional property investors, and once this concept is understood you will never see money in the same way again. I will state the patently obvious – that action is what gets results. So why do so many people not have enough passive income or recurring income to give them financial security?

Active responsibility – a new way of living

If I asked you to tell me the story of your life to date, what would you say? Would you start with the negative or positive things about your life? We all love a story – rags to riches, failure to success (though reading the newspapers sometimes I think people prefer stories describing failure rather than success).

What I believe and how I behave today is as much my story as the 'historical' fact that I used to be a university lecturer, was made redundant and had been homeless. The thoughts and beliefs I have now have shaped my life and my business – they are positively influencing my financial future.

Taking active responsibility for your financial future requires the understanding and implementation of responsibility, leverage, recurring income, action, contribution and self-preservation. I will ask you to question the way you think, even to revise what you believe, and change what you do or don't do.

This is such an important concept – it is more like my life philosophy. I have continually improved and developed it for my own purpose since I first became aware of it in 2007. I discovered the foundations of this approach to life when I went to a personal development seminar one weekend in late 2006. I started to understand how my mind worked and why I was the way I was. I learnt about critical concepts from the world of economics, psychology and neural sciences. Over the intervening years, I have brought together the thoughts and ideas of lots of philosophers, psychologists and thinkers into a personal 'soup' or recipe for success.

The first earth-shattering concept I came across was responsibility.

The underlying science is that our minds are bombarded with millions of bits of information on a nanosecond-by-nanosecond basis. We would literally go insane if we had to deal with it all on a conscious level. So, very cleverly, we have been designed to have a conscious and a subconscious brain.

As information is presented, we subconsciously *filter* it into what our mind thinks we need to know consciously and what we don't. Our breathing, the texture of the chair we're sitting on, the touch of our clothes are all dealt with on a subconscious level, unless something out of the ordinary happens. I came to understand that some of these filters are about self-preservation – like breathing and our hearts pumping.

Some filters are created to preserve us because of past experiences. For example, we don't – or not many of us – put our hands on a hot pan. This may be because our mother shouted a warning or because we burnt ourselves in the past, causing pain. The mind then protects us from doing that same or similar action again.

So everything you do (or don't do) is either consciously or subconsciously decided by you. Therefore, if you feel resistance, fear or apprehension about a certain action, it might be because somewhere in your past you had a negative feeling or warning about it, or simply lack information about it today. You might even feel resistance to this concept… are you now wondering why?

This means that everything you have or do in your life today is as a result of decisions you have or have not taken in the past. Therefore, if you are happy with your life, then it is because of you – *you* did that. If you are dissatisfied with your life, then that is also because of you – *you* did that too.

When I grasped this concept, I recognised that if everything in my life is of my doing (based on the knowledge and understanding I had at the time), then everything I want is also possible – I just have to consciously decide that I want it. This is such an empowering thought – it means I have complete control over the outcome of my life. I can design, build, have and live my life any way I want to.

You too can design, build, have and live your life – you just have to decide on the type of life you want. At this point, you can go down one of two paths: you can create a future life based on what you don't have in your life right now – seeing only the gaps; or you can choose to create a life that is grateful for everything you have and focuses on creating even more wealth, health and happiness. Which is more empowering?

The first step is to design the life you want and, sadly, 'filters' can get in the way here. Some people have negative thoughts, emotions and feelings about money, success or wealth. You weren't born like this – it was learnt from parents and peers of a past generation – people who were doing the best they could with the knowledge and resources that they had.

Some people have issues around failure and success. Sadly, much of this is taught to us in school. The aim of this book is not to teach you Neuro Linguistic Programming (NLP), as there are excellent books, courses and coaches that can do this. I do, however, recommend that you take action to address any of those 'little voices' that plague you and hold you back, otherwise they will become like balls of lead around your ankles and drag dramatically on your goals and success.

For now, I want to move forward from the concept that you can control the outcome of your life. I have decided the life I want to live – I can amend, update and even enhance this regularly throughout my life as I have new ideas and see new opportunities. This is something that you will be able to do by the end of Section 1 (if not before). I suggest that, as you feel ready, you put the book down and take out some blank paper and write whatever comes into your head – notes about what you would like to be, have or do in your life or what you imagine in your dreams. You can choose. You can enhance, improve and even rewrite your future again and again if you want as your world opens up to the possibilities that you can create.

Compounding – the art of leverage

The second concept that struck me was economics. I'm not referring to the type of economics I tried to study at school, not the supply and demand of business, although that is ever present in all of our lives whether or not we know it. I refer to economics in the form of leverage. Understanding the principle that if I have a specific number of resources (and let's use bank notes as an example), then once donated or spent they are gone from my hands. However, if I leverage (increase) those resources in some way, then I can have more bank notes in my hands which I can then donate or spend and still have my original amount left.

The following table shows the principle of doubling £1 every day for 21 days until very quickly it is over £1,000,000. Note how for the first 11 days nothing much is happening; there is no real impact of the doubling process. Then, all of a sudden, between days 17 and 21 the money starts to multiply on a massive scale.

Day	Amount (£)
1	1
2	2
3	4
4	8
5	16
6	32

7	64
8	128
9	256
10	512
11	1,024
12	2,048
13	4,096
14	8,192
15	16,384
16	32,768
17	65,536
18	131,072
19	262,144
20	524,288
21	1,048,576

My spending habits prior to understanding this principle were the same as any middle-class, reasonably well-off person, even though I was a single mum with a part-time job. If we wanted or needed something and we could afford it, we bought it. I loved to buy clothes, shoes and necklaces in particular, but I hated shopping and trying on clothes. Therefore, I would literally buy a couple of thousand pounds worth of clothes at a time on my credit card and then try them on at home in comfort with a glass of wine. I would do this two or three times a year. Did I need that many clothes or shoes? Did I wear that many clothes? Are there still boxes of brand-new shoes in my cupboard? Let's move swiftly on from that question!

What about the money – where is it? Gone, of course, and with it the opportunity to become wealthy and financially free. I had no money left to invest. I had no idea that I could or should invest. In the action of spending money on consumer items, the opportunity to leverage and create even more wealth was also spent.

In light of this knowledge, I now clearly understand that every latte, every pair of shoes, even the odd necklace has to be bought with money that has already been leveraged, with my recurring income, money I did not trade my hours for. Now when I make a purchase I am not touching my capital.

This knowledge led me to the next series of critical lessons that helped me to develop the concept of active responsibility – the power to radically take charge of your life.

Just before I discuss this topic, can I ask you to see taking charge of your life as a wonderfully positive thing? Simply put, it means you won't have to sit rocking in a urine-stained chair in some institution for the old and unwanted, or be a drain and burden on your family. You will have the power, money and freedom to choose how you live your life – right through to a very happy old age.

Recurring income – you have to work for it

I dislike the term 'passive income' because no regular income is truly passive – there still needs to be work that takes place prior to the system or asset working for you, and there still needs to be a level of monitoring and checking to keep the cash-generating machine working. This is why I prefer the phrase 'recurring income'. Recurring income is the rent that is paid into my bank account every month and I don't have to trade my time working, speaking or writing to acquire it. I do, of course, monitor and manage it though.

The important point here is to move away from trading your time for money – because that is always going to limit your growth. Even if you charge £10,000 per hour, you can still only work so many hours a day or a week. More importantly, once you have created the lifestyle that you want to live, having to trade lots of hours for money will mean that you have less time for the things you want to experience.

There are a number of ways that people can invest their resources, time, knowledge and money to create income that is not related to the trade of hours.

The stock market

This is not for me. I can't influence the value of a share and whether it's Forex or trading it still smacks of gambling to me. It lacks control and certainly does not enable me to use other people's money. No bank will give you a mortgage on a share, which might indicate that lenders do not consider them a good lending risk or an actual asset.

Internet marketing

I have definitely had a go at this over the years, but found it dull when taken out of context. It didn't require me to meet or speak to people, or indeed even to leave the house. I find those long, long sales letters boring – I don't read them and I don't understand how the research can say they work. If I could not get with the programme, then it was never going to work for me.

I will come back to this later as a brilliant form of marketing with a focus on creating websites to sell products and passion and a team of outsourcers to do the technical boring bit.

Business

Okay, business sounds do-able, although I need to be careful not to create another job for myself – this time one of managing staff. So I looked at multi-level marketing (MLM). I could see the definite benefits of leveraging other people's time as a resource. The issue for me came from the initial time it takes to build the team to that critical mass that means you don't have to work. I estimated that I would need to invest 2–3 years (depending on my initial contact database size) of my time to build and support my team to success.

During that time, I would have to work long hours for a very low rate of return. I worked out that I was earning £2.50 per hour – not a motivator for me. It is an excellent business if you already have a full-time job or you are a student looking to create a recurring income stream to buy your initial freedom. It works brilliantly if you coach people around their health and then sell products through MLM to your target group, for example.

I am not convinced though that it works for the average person looking to create an income, unless, as I mentioned, you already have a large contact database or the product is synergistic with your current business.

I actually started to invest in property straight away once I recognised that leverage was the key to financial freedom. I could see that I could borrow other people's money. In fact, I *had* to as I didn't have any savings. I could leverage any money borrowed to both pay off the cost of borrowing and still leave me with a profit. The initial capital debt would be cleared either by the sale of the asset or the later (much later) rise in asset value.

Eureka! I could design my own destiny, create my dream world and do it all without having to trade my hours. Better still, I could use other people's money and make a profit – an on-going 'recurring' income. Now all I had to do was 'do it'. Of course, this 'business' would take time to set up, but the cashflow, ROI and return on my time was almost immediate – certainly a lot quicker than with the MLM businesses.

Action – the only way to be successful

Now comes the final ingredient that takes responsibility, leverage and recurring income as concepts and turns them into a recipe for financial freedom. The ingredient is action. You can't take consistent and progressive action unless you understand how your mind works and accept the concept of responsibility. *You* are responsible for the outcomes in your life – good or bad. If you don't like the outcome, change the decision and make a better one next time. Learn from your mistakes – they are just a lesson, not something to fear.

Who would you look upon more favourably? The person who sat safely taking no risks and living a mediocre life or the person who took action, learnt, explored, got knocked down, but got up again and gave life their all – living life to their full potential and beyond?

If you take action and responsibility but you don't understand about leverage, you will spend your capital and run out of money – yours and other people's money – very quickly. If you don't understand about passive or recurring income, you will just create another job for yourself and find that you have no time to enjoy the future you dreamed of and may even have created. Time with our loved ones is precious and all too short – having fun and learning new things is the greatest gift we as humans can have. Loved ones, fun and new things will be different for all of us, but none of it will be possible if you don't take active responsibility for your life and the lives of those who depend on you.

Who are you really helping?

At this point, there are two smaller inter-linked, but still important, lessons: contribution and self-preservation. They go back to the concept of values – what is important to us in any given context. Many of us have a strong desire to help others. For some, it manifests as charity work or contribution; for others, it is 'telling' them how they can do what we have done.

I strongly believe that we have a moral duty to help others and that it is a natural instinct to help. There is a belief that the more you give, the more you get – so, if you give time, you get more time; if you give money, you attract more money; if you share your time, money, love and knowledge, you are rewarded with a truly wealthy life.

I remember being dreadfully unhappy in the final months before my marriage ended – unhappy because this was neither the life I wanted nor how I ever imagined I would be treated by another person. Even more upsetting, what sort of a role model was I for my two daughters? Did I want them to grow up and see this downtrodden miserable woman – probably unkempt as all self-confidence left her – unemployed and possibly depressed? Is that what I wanted for my two baby girls?

What had gone wrong? My mother always worked hard, supported my father and loved him. They never argued in front of me or my sister; we were a united and loving family. My mother had owned her own business before she had children and now worked for an employer, but was clearly enhancing the business with her work ethic and ideas. My father was a master tailor and ran his own business.

I remember writing 'letters' to my then husband to explain why I was unhappy – I was able to articulate it clearly in writing. It would have caused another violent argument to explain using the spoken word. I never sent the letters – it was as though I was having a conversation with another part of me that needed to make a decision, but was afraid. I needed to leave the situation, but I didn't have the knowledge and understanding that I have now. I was afraid of unseen consequences – I was responsible for two other lives and needed to make the right choice. I allowed the fear, overwhelming pressure and stress to paralyse me.

I realised that I needed to leave and started to make mental plans – working each plan out and then evaluating the consequences. Actually, I was afraid on so many levels: afraid to stay and afraid to go. In the end, the decision was taken from me and I literally nearly paid for my indecision with my life. It had taken over 18 months before circumstances – violent circumstances – stepped in and gave me a push!

When I did leave so many people helped me: friends and their friends and families. Donations of kitchen equipment or second-hand clothes for the girls were received as treasured gifts. I became so incredibly grateful that I wanted to repay the kindness – I had been given the gift of a new life.

I helped everyone (whether or not they wanted it). Everyone from the person in the queue next to me to fellow students and total strangers. I helped everyone else so much that I forgot about my daughters, whose precious lives I had set about rescuing in the first place. I forgot about my parents who supported me through incredibly difficult times. I even forgot about my father who suffered physically at the hands of my ex-husband! What about my sister and the impact on her life? How did I forget them? I was so busy giving my time and attention to everyone else rather than focusing on those people nearest to me who loved me.

I spent close to the next 10 years helping 'others' (mostly the students and businesses I worked with at the university) achieve their goals, dreams and desires and did nothing to directly support my family towards greater financial security and happiness. Why? Because my values were all about giving back and supporting others to have the opportunity I was given – the opportunity of a new and wonderful life.

I first heard the story of the aeroplane oxygen masks at a seminar in 2007. On an aeroplane, the hostess explains that in the event of an accident the oxygen masks will fall from the compartment overhead. She tells you to put on your own mask first. If we did not hear that instruction, the natural instinct for many of us would be to check on others around us first. Does that resonate with you? What would you do?

In fact, if you stop to help others before ensuring your own air supply, you may well pass out and die. If you put on your own mask (financial or oxygen-giving) first, then you can help the 6–10 people around you and they can help the 6–10 around them. In fact, by putting on your own mask first you could save the whole plane!

The second interwoven complexity is that in our desire to help we can be prone to 'telling', to sharing the results of our lessons in the honest attempt to help others not make mistakes. We need to remember that everyone has their own values; everyone has their own unique pasts and their own unique futures. Not everyone will be at the same point in their journey of life as you, not even your own family, especially brothers and sisters.

People need to travel at their own speed. If you are moving more swiftly to financial security and financial freedom, leave the door open for others to follow. Let them see the path you have taken so they can follow when they are ready. We all have to learn our own lessons. How many times did you sit in school and hear the teacher and understand the lesson, but know that people around you hadn't – or vice versa?

So, while we may have grasped the concept of active responsibility and know what we have to do to put it into action, others around us will not be able to take that step. They may lack the courage to overcome their fears or they may not be prepared to examine the beliefs that underlie their core values and create their results. We don't need to boast, brag or show off – we just need to be congruent and get on with living the dream life that we have created for ourselves and our immediate families. Then, when others are ready, you (the teacher) will be there, prepared to share all of your knowledge so that others may learn from your mistakes and successes, helping them to create their own version of a wonderful life.

Changing the future for our children's children

Our schools are failing our children and future generations on so many levels – I could write a book on that subject alone. To summarise, at a basic level, the system is failing to teach even reading, writing and maths skills – core skills for any sort of future. At another level, there is no financial education whatsoever to prepare our young people for the real world. Children are theoretically being trained to be employees without an understanding of the geo-political-economic environment they are entering. As employees, they could add so much to any business if they understood world economics. Why? Because, unlike many of us, they understand the emerging new uses of technology – the interconnectedness of everything – so much better.

Schools train our kids to be employees – if they stay the course and learn the basics. That's not so bad because not everyone is ready to be an entrepreneur and run their own business. Many want the security of a job and we need people to serve us in the shops and heal us when we're sick. It might be nice if people could choose. Maybe those who don't feel that school or employment is a path for them would benefit from knowing that they have other options. Maybe they would recognise that self-employment, entrepreneurship or investment is the answer they are searching for.

What is criminal is not explaining to young people how money works and how to leverage it. When my daughter moved into her first home she understood the techniques of a professional investor because I viewed the first few properties with her and explained, in context, how to offer, how to know what to offer, what research to do, what to look for and what questions to ask.

More importantly, she knows that she will never sell this house. When she is ready to trade up, she will release equity and then rent this property to professional tenants because she has bought in the right location. My daughter understands that she can take her current savings and leverage them for her own purpose. She understands about assets and liabilities. She understands about good debt and bad debt. She understands how to use credit cards to build credit ratings and not to make others rich by paying massive interest rates.

It is your *duty* to prepare your children for the world because school and the educational system will not. Explain the principles you have read in this chapter:

- You can do anything you set your mind to – you have the power to decide your future.

- Once £1 is spent, it is gone for good – leverage and spend from revenue or capital gains.

- You can have a job and still create other income on the side – you can have a MLM business or internet business – you could write a book, create a product or offer another service.

- The 'system' is crumbling, therefore, you must take active responsibility for your financial future – government cannot sustain a free education, healthcare and welfare system, and pensions are linked to a fluctuating stock market that government has no control over.

- There is good debt and bad debt, assets and liabilities. Learn the difference.

- When you want to learn something new, seek out someone who is doing it now, is being successful and is relevant. Not someone who did something in a different financial or economic climate that is worlds apart from now.

Lastly, I once heard a great talk where the speaker said that in every family there is a cycle of wealth. A generation that labours hard to create real money that the next generation uses and invests to create a recurring income. Then comes the third generation that is born into a wealthy family with no relationship to the money it relies upon and spends it – effectively losing it all.

I believe we go through that cycle as a country and an economy, but the cycles are moving faster. It is our job to *educate* our children and our children's children about money – how it works, how it flows. We all need to learn to tap into the rivers of money flowing around in our economy and make it work for us. How exactly we do that will change – originally it changed within a generation, then it changed within a decade and now it changes almost annually!

Teach your family about real money and relative money (see page 69). Teach them how to leverage, not to save. Teach them how passive income works and that it is not passive, it is in fact recurring income – because it needs love and attention to keep working.

Chapter 2

It's time to think about thinking

Every so often I decide to get off the work treadmill for a couple of weeks and to clear my diary. It often feels as if I am so involved in my businesses, so close to them, that I can no longer see where I am going without this enforced distance. I know what I want to achieve, and I like to check I am heading in the right direction.

By encouraging you to slow down and even take a break from business for a couple of weeks, this chapter will show you how to tap into untold energy, focus and direction. I will explain the mechanical process, unravel some of the science and explain the results.

This chapter will explain how:

- aligning your values with your business goals will virtually guarantee success, without anything else coming into play

- listening for and looking for messages from your subconscious is a path to opportunity and success

- to filter for success and retrain your 'little voice' to be more supportive

- writing your goals is a great tool to train your mind to focus on what you want to achieve.

Ultimately, you can choose whether or not you change your thinking but, as Henry Ford's wise saying goes, 'If you always do what you've always done, then you'll always get what you've always got'. If you are happy with your results so far, then great! However, I imagine that you are reading this book because you want to achieve even more success, wealth and happiness and that is going to require a change in thinking.

Life is getting faster, time is getting shorter. We rush to achieve and succeed. When do we make time to think and plan? This chapter is about thinking rather than planning – the stage that needs to come before planning. If you miss out the thinking stage of the planning process, then how will you know if you have considered the potential consequences of what you might be planning?

The mechanical process

When I first decided to become an author I knew what I wanted it to be about. What I didn't understand was how the book would fit into my business and, if it did, what that meant. My primary business is sourcing property, so why did I want to write a book? I decided that I needed some time to think – a period of relaxation and quiet contemplation.

That already sounds a bit strange. Actually, it was days crossed out in my diary when I could think, read, listen and learn instead of just doing all the time. It could be called 'strategic development', a very corporate sounding process. It is actually the art of thinking about your business – some working *on* it time rather than working *in* it.

The mechanical process that took place was easy – I crossed out three weeks in my diary and pledged to not make any appointments or meetings during that time. This was going to be time where I could 'choose' to do what I wanted rather than fulfil business-based 'obligations'. That is actually the key to the success of the process: choice not obligation; space and time not meetings and appointments. You need to be committed and strict with yourself, otherwise the outside world will creep in and steal your thinking time.

When I had my first 'business retreat' ideas flowed into (or out of) my head at a phenomenal rate and quality – a really 'mysterious process' and an unusual feeling. I often have ideas, but these were clear, inspired, ground-breaking business and life-altering realisations.

What I had created was the space and time for my poor subconscious mind to share bits of information and ideas that it had filed away as not dramatically important in the moment they were experienced or thought. I allowed ideas to flow into my head. (From where they came: the super conscious, other minds, other lives, or just the energy that surrounds – I did not know.) As the pace of life slowed and the diary quietened, I could think more easily. I could hear my thoughts in the silence and they were good ideas! My thoughts helped me to see strategies and opportunities to grow my business.

What's important to you? You can choose what you value

I first studied NLP in 2007 and, as mentioned in Chapter 1, I have identified what I believe to be the three critical business skills needed to drive your business to the next level.

If you have read around this subject or been to events embodying NLP practice, then you will understand the concepts of 'values, attitudes and beliefs' and how they impact on our daily lives and how our subconscious mind operates a 'life-saving' filtering process to keep us safe and sane. If this is all news to you, then please explore this concept.

I learnt that we can either live our lives at the effect, direction and impact of others, or we can take active responsibility for the decisions we make and change those that produce outcomes we do not desire.

Ultimately, you are responsible for everything that happens in your life, not your boss, parent, the government or the other driver – *you are responsible*. This is such an empowering realisation. You can choose to do anything you want, be anything you want, have anything you want – and change it if you don't like it!

Values are the traits and qualities that are important to you. When I first did this exercise, I realised that my values were all about helping other people, sharing and supporting. These are great qualities, yet they did not seem to help *my* family. This is why the air hostess story is such an important metaphor. '…put on your own mask first' – the choice is save yourself and then the 6–10 people around you or pass out trying to help the person closest to you.

I realised that success, wealth and finances were not something that I had listed as important to me. With the support of my coach, I was able to change my thoughts and the things I valued. I will mention coaching later but, at this point, I want to emphasise how a good coach can dramatically impact on your success. As I gradually let go of limiting beliefs that held me back, my coaching sessions have changed emphasis and now hold me accountable for the goals I set.

Changing the way I thought and what I valued, in turn, changed my subconscious filtering mechanism – did I 'see' more opportunities or 'attract' them to me? I don't know. Within three weeks, I won a contract for £20,000 from a past contact. Within eight months, I had trained and bought my first investment property. Within 18 months, I was financially free! That is why understanding your values, getting them aligned and supporting your goals is crucial to your business and personal success. This is why getting the right coach can help support that process of change. I now have the honour of performing this role with my mentees.

Aligning your values to your goals virtually guarantees success. A famous proverb states: 'A true warrior has all his horses face the same direction.' Your values are a critical part of your cavalry.

Messages – what is your subconscious trying to tell you?

I can't remember when I first read *The Celestine Prophecy* by James Redfield. It's a story about a man on a journey and how he learns to recognise signs and messages in the things that happen around him. Signs and messages from whom? Actually, it's more scientific than mystical. Remember, our senses are bombarded with information overload. To remain sane our subconscious mind filters this information so we don't have to consciously think to breathe or pump blood around our bodies. In the filtering process we may miss things, so our subconscious 'notices' signs, symbols, even words or music that might trigger a memory of something that passed us by unnoticed at a conscious level.

Our mind is such a wonderful and powerful tool, we just don't pay it enough attention. Sometimes 'messages' appear as a vague sense of awareness, other times we seem to 'see' the same thing over and over again. People repeat patterns in work or relationships and ask the question 'is this a message?' when they get the same results. Well, the answer is 'yes'.

Celebrity or success – what are you filtering for?

Lots of people read celebrity magazines, which have fuelled a whole media industry. So where in their filtering process did the message that 'success is desirable' become replaced with the message that 'celebrity is desirable'? What made people value celebrity? Maybe somewhere in their thinking patterns people have confused celebrity status (whatever that means) as an indicator of success and, to some maybe, it is the same thing.

Most of the general public read about the lives of people who marry and have babies, face lifts or public disputes. You, however, are most likely reading about how key business people created their businesses and overcame challenges to shape their thinking and achieve financial freedom. That is what sets you apart. Your filtering process is different. You value different things to the ordinary person on the street. You have created different rules about what is important to you (whether or not you are aware of this).

Now you can enhance that process and specifically filter for certain behaviours, traits or achievements by influencing your values, writing your goals and directing your education.

What are the voices telling you?

Limiting beliefs or the concept of 'the little voice' is an NLP principle. The idea is that we all hear a voice (or voices) in our head. If you are asking 'what voice?', then that *is* the voice. Sometimes it can be negative or limiting. Ultimately, it is only doing its best to protect you.

The voices will kick in when the filtering process fails. If you either recognise an opportunity or fail to recognise something that might 'harm' you in some way, then the little voice will have to take charge and make clear any underlying fears or concerns.

Again, aligning your focus and values will help you to train your subconscious to know what is important to you. Writing your goals will make clear what you want to achieve. The process of thinking about and writing down your goals takes time, focus and thought. Your subconscious notices this as a significant activity and that ultimately impacts on what you value, filter and focus on. This can even help to quieten some of the more negative voices or limiting beliefs and sharpen your filtering process to recognise opportunities.

What did you dream about last night?

The inner voices can also come to us in our dreams; here, it appears as images rather than words (although some people may have words in their dreams too). Dream analysis is a tool that enables you to analyse the remembered contents of a dream. It can be used as a specific tool to communicate with the subconscious part of our brains. Keep a notepad by your bed and then first thing in the morning make a note of what you remember, you might be able to start to see the messages that your subconscious wants to send you.

Now I am not sure what will come first: the chicken or the egg. In other words, I don't know if you will start to recognise opportunities and answers to challenges because you follow this process, or if by following this process you open a channel of communication with the subconscious mind. I don't think it matters as long as you gain a deeper understanding of something you previously didn't understand.

You don't have to understand everything I have just covered: from values and beliefs, limiting little voices, dream analysis or communicating with your subconscious through signs and dreams, goal writing and coaching – you might not even need to believe it all. Just be open to the idea that there are things that we don't completely understand. Having said this, these new ways of thinking (NLP and beyond) do have provable results. My life has changed dramatically since I decided to be open to these ideas – take them on board, test them out with an open mind and create my own recipe for success. Now you just need to take action on what you have learnt.

Bringing our thinking together

If you add all of this new understanding together, what you will have learnt is that there is a body of thought (or belief system) that believes there are three levels of consciousness:

1. Our conscious mind, which may decide to have a cup of tea rather than coffee; it has the ability to make conscious choices.
2. Our unconscious or subconscious mind, which controls our survival – from breathing through to flight or fight responses. This part of our brain also subconsciously influences our decisions. This may manifest itself as our inability to make a decision or take an action. It can also migrate into our conscious world as a voice that says: 'I wouldn't do that if I were you, it will only go wrong…'; 'you don't deserve to be successful – you never have been before…'; or it might appear as a garbled message in a remnant of a half-remembered dream.
3. Our super conscious, which sits outside our body; it is the collection of all that is and all that was. (I admit I don't fully understand all there is to know on this topic. However, I remain open and inquisitive about the concept.)

The best bit is that I have worked out why I sometimes resist certain decisions or actions. By being in tune with my subconscious mind, listening, thinking and analysing, I have been able to regain control over my life. This is something that you can achieve easily. One way is to accept that there were things you didn't know about before and you have simply become more vigilant and attentive for any messages.

If this topic area intrigues you as I know it will, then check out the resources on the website that accompanies this book, and do some reading on the subject for yourself. Develop your own understanding – it may be different from mine because you may need to put emphasis on a different part of the thinking process.

What are the practical applications of all this thinking?

It boils down to three key points for me:

1. By acknowledging that I have a little voice (in my case, a whole choir of voices) in my head and by listening out for them, I can start to tell when I am taking an action that at some level unsettles or scares me. By recognising this, I can think consciously about it and even double-check the decision. This is a very positive thing to do – self-affirming and appropriate. Once I am sure that I want to pursue that particular action, then I can acknowledge my inner voice and thank it for helping me and take appropriate action.
2. When I face a challenge or become stuck for inspiration, I can use dream analysis. Then trust that I will understand what action I need to take next.
3. I am alert to new learning and opportunities in my daily life. Again, these might be things that my subconscious mind has noticed or wants to share with me. That is why all my blogs contain stories with messages – because I see them everywhere. My focus is clear. My aim is to develop even further my successful cashflowing property business and so my subconscious wants to help me in any way it can by pointing out things that will act as reminders, memory triggers and potential opportunities.

What new understanding could you tap into if you became more alert for signs that you had missed subconsciously in amongst the mass of information? What business opportunity, strategy or person could you connect with? What greater clarity and drive towards your goals could you achieve if your whole mind is working towards the same outcome?

I can remember my mother telling me that I think too much. My 'thought' is that, if you know what you want and believe, your thoughts can help you to achieve your goals. Can you ever think too much? Can you ever achieve too much?

We only understand and use less than 10% of our brain. Who is to say that any of what I have written is not true? If you can start to understand how you think and why you think the way you do…, if you can start to get your whole mind and body working together like a well-oiled machine, you could become an Olympic athlete in your own business.

After we have:

- understood our thought processes
- recognised and mastered the little voice and so removed our limiting beliefs
- adopted empowering values and beliefs
- connected and worked in harmony with our whole minds
- analysed our dreams
- taken responsibility for our decisions and their outcomes
- learnt to leverage our resources

…the final component to all of this thinking is, of course,

- to take action.

The book by Jeff Olson, *The Slight Edge,* was amazing – it was written just for me. (Or it felt like it when I read it for the first time.) The author spoke of the compounding effect of making the 'right' decisions. It brought together the idea that I can influence and control my own future with the power of leverage. It reminded me that, from day to day, it is hard to see the progress that has been made, but as we look back from the future we can see the massive distances we have travelled.

I am a whole new person since I started this journey. I'm not different – more rediscovered – I remember all my forgotten possibilities. All that I am now was always my potential. I had allowed others to steal my power, confidence, passion and determination. Starting at school with teachers saying I asked too many questions, to the bullying by other pupils, then to work colleagues and their spiteful gossip, through to unsupportive and disempowering employers, and finally to an ex-husband!

Now I know what I want to achieve. I know that I can achieve it on my own and even more quickly with the support and collaboration of the wonderful people by whom I am surrounded. Above all, my journey is my choice. I am powerful beyond measure and humbled by that knowledge.

I really want this chapter to enable you to see that you, too, are powerful beyond measure. Be humbled by that knowledge and then continue reading – pulling out vital pieces of knowledge or experience that will help you to speed along a less bumpy pathway to your financial freedom.

Chapter 3

From thinking to doing

Until now, I have hardly mentioned property investment other than as a casual frame of reference. This is because I spent a whole year before I was even ready to consider property investing gaining the basics of the knowledge and understanding I have just been discussing.

Well, that's not totally true because if I look back (isn't hindsight a wonderful thing?), I can see that property investment was a clear message or calling throughout my adult life, from working for a mortgage broker to looking at the differences between new build and older constructions and how people could leverage the value of certain properties over and above normal inflation rates. Even so, it still took many years of debate and discussion before I eventually took action, and then it was only to engage a sourcing agent to help me!

I certainly was not engaged at this point. I still was not doing anything about creating my own financial security because I simply did not have that as a concept I could even consider. I just gave a man our money and was lucky that he picked great investments for us.

That is why I work with my clients to develop their investment strategy so that they are engaged in the process. It is their responsibility because the wealth I help them to access will determine the shape of their future lives.

Once I understood this and then continued with my education around wealth, finances and the economy, I was ready to use property investment as my vehicle to financial freedom. Alongside gaining knowledge, both mental and technical, I was imagining my ideal lifestyle, my dream life. I knew how much money I needed to live that life and I knew what my days would be like – how I would spend my time. I created a picture and then added detail – I still add detail. That gave me my reason to invest in property. It gives me strength to overcome the inevitable challenges of doing something different to everyone else. It helps me to stay motivated and focused.

This chapter is going to take you on a journey. It will help you to map out your future, decide your financial needs, reach equilibrium and recognise how valuable your time is. By the end, you will have the outline of your personal financial strategy – the vital first step to creating your property business – to give you the strength to blast through the obstacles and challenges that may come to test your resolve.

The critical success factor in any business venture is your ability to keep going when others stop. That is of course providing you are on a path to success and have chosen the right strategies. I will cover the technical detail of property investing and running a successful property investment business in greater depth later on in this book in Section 3.

What does your cake look like?

I will use the analogy of a recipe (it must be lunchtime while I am writing). If you don't know what sort of cake you want to bake, then how do you know if you have the right ingredients? Come to think of it, are you even following a recipe that is relevant to you now? For example, if you want to eat more healthily or avoid wheat, is the recipe you are following going to give you the outcome you want?

Okay, so let's start from the beginning. What do you want your cake to look like – your life to look like? Are you interested in outdoor activities, travel, country living? Do you want to ease future financial pressures when your children go to university or you retire? Whatever you choose is fine; it is your life and your future. Just make sure it is *your* life and *your* future and not about buying a house for a relative. The reason I mention this takes us back to the concept of helping others. When I started investing, I did what many of you may be thinking about… I decided to buy my parents a new house in the country. When I actually spoke to my mother and asked her what she wanted, she said she didn't want to move!

This brings us to a section in the book where you need to be totally selfish for a few pages and put your needs above others. Focus on just *your* goals. Then you can add in contribution and wider family later.

So, if you have chosen *your* end goal (which may grow, develop and change before you even get there because you can make it even better if you want), what are a few of the steps you need to take along the way?

Now you have created an end goal you will need some interim goals to get you there – this is not so hard. My biggest dream is to dive in all of the warm water coral reefs of the world taking wonderful photographs and learning about the natural life of the sea. Photographs and marine biology were added to my dream as I started to develop my vision. This vision is actually a metaphor for a whole lifestyle needed to support it.

One of my business partners wants a donkey. A donkey to keep some horses company in a field at the back of his large house where he lives the life of his dreams with his family. The donkey is his metaphor – the anchor for his vision.

Now that I had my vision (my cake) I started to work out how much money I had coming in and how much I needed to live this lifestyle. I calculated very roughly what the shortfall was – this became my financial goal or, to stay with the metaphor, the 'shopping list of ingredients' I needed.

How much money do you really need?

Now I had a figure in mind. Initially, it was a rather easy and conservative number to achieve, but enough to buy me four scuba-diving holidays a year, along with a few UK-based long weekends for good measure. My initial personal target was £120,000 per annum.

It is all well and good to create targets of £1,000,000 per year, but I believe a realistic plan to achieve that would take a considerable time. Can you sustain your drive long enough to achieve it?

Look at the figure of £120,000 – that is £10,000 per month. That could be 40 properties giving £250 net profit per month on an assured shorthold tenancy (AST). It could be renovating and flipping a property every three months for £30,000 profit. It could be sourcing two properties a month for bespoke clients. Or it could be a combination of all of the above. All of this is achievable but still a stretch.

Each time I get close to my financial target and I feel my performance dropping, I revise the goal and stretch it further. If you set a goal for £1,000,000 per annum, you will need a staff team and a massive business to manage it. I want to scuba dive and spend time with Bob, my partner, and my family and friends – not sit at a computer or in an office managing a business. If you do, then that's fine. Think about the life you want to live as well as the money and make sure the two can work together in harmony.

Finding your financial equilibrium

Another process I went through was to make sure I understood my own current and immediate financial situation. Did our family income meet or exceed our expenses? Were our expenses as a family reasonable? Was every bill necessary? I realised that we were paying for an old decreasing term life insurance policy that still cost £65 per month, but would now only pay out a fraction of our mortgage. We also had four other life and health policies. So, after a careful review of our insurance needs, I cancelled a number of policies, including a family health care policy that included the girls but no longer provided them with cover. I saved £455 per month. That's just under two good buy-to-let property cashflows! I have already mentioned that I learnt about leverage and so changed my spending habits. This saved another £500 per month on average.

Next, I looked at our credit cards, credit reports and credit scores. By using a 0% strategy, I saved money and, in fact, made money.

All of this research led me to a point where I understood our financial position. I also started to understand how money worked and flowed. I knew the life I wanted to live and how much money it would take to get there. I knew what I wanted my days to be like – how much time I was prepared to spend to maintain, sustain and enhance our wealth in the future. Now I could start to think about the technicalities of which strategy to pursue.

Understand why you want to invest in property. What image or dream is going to keep you going through the tough times? What is going to help you face the inevitable challenges that will come across your path to financial freedom? Knowledge, determination and focusing on success are what separate the successful investor from the ordinary person in the street.

Case study – from fearing redundancy to a life in the country

A mum of two was holding down two jobs to make ends meet. Her main employer was looking to make staff redundant and she hated her job. In fact, she recently told me that she realised it was 'killing' her. She already had some properties, but there was no equity and a negative cashflow, causing an even bigger leak in the family budget.

Her dream was to not have to work, to focus on her art and her children and, if possible, to move out of London. I helped her buy four cashflowing properties, restructure her finances and let out her residential home so that she could then buy another house out of London and change the quality of life for her family.

She knew what she didn't want and by working together we created her dream. I used my knowledge and understanding to act as a catalyst that ultimately changed her life. We still stay in touch and she regularly lets me know how amazing her life is, how happy she is and how much happier her children are. She took active responsibility for her life, understood leverage and took action – now she has the rest – the life of her dreams. We are already making plans to buy her a few more properties.

What you focus on is what you get

I have already explained that property investing was ringing so loudly in my ears that I had no choice other than to open the door to those possibilities. I have also explained why I do not pursue other business and investment models and part of that reason, or rather the major part, is focus.

There is a saying 'Focus on One Course Until Successful' (FOCUS). I spent many months explaining to my coach that I was focused. When he raised my lack of focus as a possible reason I was not getting the success I wanted, I argued back that I was like a juggler – I had three balls in the air, but at any one time I was only focused on the ball at the top of the cycle. Quite good I thought...

Months later, when I was miserable and still not achieving the success I wanted, I surrendered and it really did feel like that. I focused only on buying cashflowing property in one area in the north west of England – one strategy. I was scared – was I missing other opportunities? Everything I had tried before wasn't giving me the results I wanted, so I had to give this 'focus thing' a chance. Maybe focus really was just one thing?

Everything changed. During 2009, on average I bought one or two houses per month. I also set up my first property-related business – a sourcing service for bespoke clients who had access to equity or savings but neither the time nor knowledge to invest in property themselves. I earned an additional £17,500 in sourcing fees and 'ready to invest' strategy development sessions. Focus was working for me – my surrender had paid off.

I speak to so many potential property investors and they all tell me how they are dabbling in other money-making opportunities. Some are doing rent-to-rent, a bit of internet marketing or they trade stocks. Chapter 1 explains about filtering out the overwhelming amounts of 'normal' information our brains have to cope with... yet some people are increasing their load. Our minds are already being overwhelmed with information, why load it with even more?

One young guy told me proudly how he had just completed on his first deal and now owned a cashflowing property. I asked him what he was going to do next (either buy more properties or source deals was the answer I expected). His reply was 'trade on the stock market'. He found something that worked and so, instead of doing it again and being successful again, he was going to start another new business model!?

In 2010, when I wrote my first book, my property buying rate dropped to one property a month. In 2011, when I developed my training business, I bought five properties in seven months. I definitely shop for property at a better rate when I am single-minded about it!

I have identified a cashflowing model – all I need to do is repeat it. As soon as you find your model, do it again and again. You need to develop a deeper understanding and knowledge in your model to become an expert. That expertise will enable you to reach your goal either by leveraging your money or by helping you to leverage other people's money for a fee. To change business models before you become financially secure seems like madness to me.

I do recognise that some people buy their first property and then realise that they don't enjoy it. If this is the case, I would suggest that you suffer for another year or two and build a portfolio that creates the financially secure platform from which you can develop any business and create any life you like. This is why your 'why' needs to be so powerful and compelling to help you stay focused.

I will say that it would be no different if you are Sir Richard Branson, Warren Buffet or Lord Alan Sugar. Why? Because, although they now have massive teams of people to support them, they all started out on their own, focused on their own personal cash-creating strategy. They stuck with it, until they were successful!

Diversification is a good thing once you have achieved financial freedom. Once you have the money, time, knowledge, systems and team to support you, then you can diversify.

A key part in my ability to achieve the level of focus needed to be successful was having someone to whom I was accountable, my mentor. Even though I had created a powerful 'why', a powerful and compelling vision of my dream life, I still needed support – a mentor to guide me on my path. I jokingly have described myself as having obsessive compulsive disorder (OCD) combined with attention deficit disorder (ADD), in that I was completely focused on my goal and the tasks in hand until some shining opportunity caught my attention and distracted me. To be honest I still have the same problem – too many good ideas and opportunities but now I have my team and together we stay on target and focused.

What shining possibility is taking your attention off your goal? What is delaying your journey to financial freedom?

Who is holding you accountable and helping you maintain the focus you need? If you are resisting this question, then you are not focused now and I bet you are not financially free either!

Case study – sometimes what you focus on is not what you want

For over a year, one of my client's efforts and attention were on property investment. For various technical reasons, the strategy was not working and the deserved success was not forthcoming. My client was working diligently 30 hours a week and was very successful to a point, but never quite closed the deal. Months later, it became clear that they were not following their passion. Their passion was to help others. This was their core value. They have now established a successful and inspiring coaching practice.

Sometimes we have to acknowledge that what we think we want to do, might not be our best idea. Sometimes what we start doing is someone else's perfect idea, and we copied them.

> **Case study – sometimes what you focus on is what you want; you just don't realise it**
>
> Four weeks into one of my group mentoring programmes there was still resistance and a lack of results for one man with a clear vision of why he wanted to invest in property. He saw sourcing as the business model he could use to enhance his capital pot. Then came the breakthrough. The client realised that they wanted to pursue property through a different strategy – they really felt they wanted to buy and sell property as they had a limiting belief about the size of their capital pot and ability to attract funding. Their focus shifted and everything fell into line. They are now in the process of completing on their first deal. The real irony is that having achieved their first deal they can see how easy it is – they are now in the process of developing a sourcing business again and have attracted other private investors.
>
> Sometimes all it takes is time and patience to realise what will help you achieve your goals as easily as possible. There is a fine line between following someone's dream and remaining determined to achieve your own!

Mentoring – what's good, what's bad?

Committing to a coaching programme is an essential business need. Finding the right mentor is the difference between success and a longer path! As with training courses, carry out a skills analysis – think about what you want to achieve. What skills do you need to be successful? What do you *honestly* have and what do you need help with? Who is successful in your industry? What is their story? When and how did they start? Be careful if they built their fortune using remortgaging, NMD strategies, as they may not have the relevant experience to help someone who is starting in a more conservative lending market.

When you identify the right person for you, make sure each session has a purpose, topic or challenge that needs resolving and discussing. It is all too easy to spend your time chatting or, worse, moaning. Make sure there is a structure to your sessions – ask about this upfront. Is this the structure that you want? Will it help you to achieve your goals?

Don't be afraid to end your sessions and choose another coach. This doesn't have to be because the first coach failed – hopefully it is because you outgrew them. When I work with a client, my aim is to make myself redundant. Then I know I have done a good job.

Have different mentors for different things. I have a mentor who helps me when I reach each new entrepreneurial edge and I am about to take a massive step to change my business. I also have mentors who I use for sales training, property knowledge and business coaching. Look around – ask people and then get the right business mentor – fit for your purpose.

Money matters

If this whole chapter is about making the transition from theory into real world business decisions, then money clearly matters and understanding how to use it as a tool is vital. Take credit cards – if you are going to use credit cards, you must understand the difference between good debt and bad debt, interest rates and of course leverage. I explain more about what lenders want in Chapter 5 on page 79. Right now, let's look at leverage using credit cards.

You can use a credit card to buy something you want – this could even be a property – and then pay off the credit card debt through monthly instalments. If you haven't mastered the proper technique, you will be paying interest on that debt, which will take you a lot longer to clear and be more expensive than a mortgage.

Alternatively, you can get a credit card offer for a balance transfer at 0%. (This usually comes with a 3% fee but over a year this is still cheap money.) Depending on the lender, this can be spent or transferred into a bank account. Imagine if you could get £20,000 spread over two or three credit cards all at 0% and then use that money to fund a property purchase. The property could give you £200–£250 per month net cashflow, which would pay off the monthly credit card costs. Then, in a year's time, remortgage the property, release the equity (which may or may not equal the credit card bill) and clear the card (or refinance at 0% again if you have to). Now the property will give more cashflow. None of this was your money – you leveraged available resources.

Are you a homeowner with a 'drawdown mortgage facility'? This is an agreement that you can borrow money against the value of your house when you need it and repay it without penalty. Examples of this include some Woolwich mortgages, First Direct, Virgin or Halifax One accounts.

If you have sufficient equity, you can 'draw down' or borrow against your home, buy an investment property, refurbish, remortgage and repay the money back to your mortgage account. You will have then bought a property with none of your own money all totally legally. You could have £200–£300 extra cashflow per month. What if you keep repeating this process? These are some of the strategies I discuss in my first book, *Using Other People's Money*.

If you are going to start using money (other people's money), then you must understand interest and ROI. ROI or cash-on-cash returns is a way of measuring just how much the money you are using is earning. This can be compared to banks' interest rates or the costs of borrowing the original capital sums.

The formula is simple:

- Above the dividing line is the net profit from the investment. So, in the example of buying a buy-to-let property, above the line is the annual net rent. This is the gross rent from the tenant minus the letting agent fees, the mortgage and, I believe, the property insurance, because without paying the mortgage or the property insurance you can't have the money to buy the house in the first place.

- Below the dividing line are all the cash costs needed to get the property to a point where it produces rent. So the deposit on the property (20–25%), the solicitor, surveyor and broker fees, costs to refurbish the property, gas certificates, tenant search fees (without which you wouldn't have a tenant to pay rent) and, when sourcing for a bespoke client, my sourcing fee (which is another cost incurred when buying the property because without my help you would not have that specific deal).

- When you divide the smaller top number by the larger bottom number you will get a figure less than one. Maybe 0.10 or anything from 0.04–0.35 – this is effectively a percentage (10, 4 or 35%). This means that this investment would earn you that percentage income, and so you can compare that to the less risky interest offered by the savings accounts or the cost of borrowing the money to fund the investment. ROI is explained further in Chapter 8 from page 129.

You can use this information to calculate potential profit shares or payments to joint venture partners. This is a much more realistic measure to calculate the difference between two investment opportunities as it includes all costs, rather than yield which only divides gross rent by actual purchase price.

The last thing to consider is to never give up the day job! Without a regular salary, you will not be able to get a mortgage and then all of this is mute. Someone in your investment team – your husband, girlfriend or brother – has to work and earn a sufficient salary to meet the lenders' criteria. For example, some lenders want you to earn over £24,000 per annum as a second surety against the rent not coming in. Money matters – know where yours is coming from, how much it costs and what it will earn you!

Time matters

Once you take on an entrepreneurial spirit and lifestyle, the old nine-to-five mentality seems strange, unnatural even. You become passionate and enthusiastic about what you are doing – something lots of employees fail to experience. Unfortunately, what also happens is that you forget to value your time!

I think this is what makes me most frustrated when I speak to other investors or to clients. They can talk about all the things they are doing to find a deal, the adverts, the number of clever marketing activities, the conversations with 'potential vendors' (especially those doing lease options). Yet, when they talk about the 'returns' they are making, the deals they are transacting, they are spending lots of time for very little cash return. Some are earning less than the £2.50 an hour!

My question is how many hours of work do you need to put into a strategy before you have a cast-iron deal that will generate cashflow? If you have a brilliant system that filters out those 'potential' deals and leaves you working on live deals that conclude within 4–8 weeks, then great. You need to understand that the time you spend needs to generate a wage to pay for your cost of living. So how much time you take to complete a deal needs to be rewarded by the size of the cashflow.

The principle is simple. How much time did you spend to earn how much money? What is the return on your time invested (ROTI) in the deal – cash for time cost? Then, divide one into the other and you have your hourly rate. I worked this out with one client and they spent a year earning £200 per month. Yes, I know there are back end 'potential' pay outs when in three, five or seven years you finalise the deal (*if* you can, *if* the economic situation and *if* the lending situation enables it). Meantime, you still have to eat, pay your home costs and your utility bills.

When the strategy you are following does not tie in with your financial goals and provide the income stream you need quickly, then how can you sustain that strategy without moving into debt? (Unless, of course, you planned to have a whole year's income in your cashflow account to support yourself during this time!) The key to success in property in my opinion is answering the question: how can you make money from your property knowledge as quickly as possible? You will need to be congruent and ethical to have a long-term, stress-free future. You will need to work hard!

If you were to source one deal for a £2,000 fee once a month, would that help? What about one deal at £5,000 every other month? Could you scale that up once you had your system worked out?

Cash rich or cash poor?

Now what if you were to start again and make money this time? How much money would you need a month to cover expenses? How much would you need to become financially secure – or even financially free?

The crucial place to start is with your income and expenses. If expenses exceed income, then you are in trouble straight away – even if it is just by £250 per month that's £3,000 debt after one year. When I first took a look at our income and expenses (we were still working but I was being made redundant – so I thought I would check), we were doing okay. What I noticed was how many old insurance policies we had, medical cover, life, etc. and then subscriptions for magazines we had no time to read!

I checked our new insurance requirements and the paperwork carefully and then cancelled everything unnecessary and unused. What are you paying for that is unnecessary? If your expenses exceed your income, you might need to move beyond looking at just the direct debits in your bank account and look at your actual spending habits. I have a spreadsheet that I share with clients to help them record all of their spending. Complete this, or a similar, spreadsheet for a month – for the whole family – and see what you are spending your money on.

I heard a brilliant explanation of people's spending habits. Robert Kiyosaki said that your expenses are like a forecast on your future: 'What you spend on now is what you will get in the future.' If you spend your money on coaching, personal development and wealth creation, then you will get wealthy. If you spend your money on shoes, you will get a packed wardrobe. If you spend your money on take-away meals and computer games, you will get a big a_ _ _! (I leave you to fill in the blanks.)

The temptation is to spiral into blame and argument, especially if money is a stressor in your house (either for you alone or for your family). Remember, money is a resource that needs managing, monitoring and, above all, leveraging!

Once you know whether you are in equilibrium or in debt, then you can start to make informed decisions.

How much are you worth?

Even without the information from the family budget spreadsheet, you can still work out how much you are worth. However, I believe that you need all of the information and you can draft these figures now and then use the spreadsheet to confirm or amend your true spending habits.

Once you know your monthly outgoings, you know the baseline figure that you need to generate in order to meet expenses. Let's assume £2,500 is the baseline figure, as this will cover the outgoings that the majority of families experience (please do use your own figures if you prefer). Please note that I am not going to work out tax, etc. Let's just keep the numbers simple for the purposes of this exercise. £2,500 per month means £30,000 per annum (2500 x 12).

Now, as a professional investor, you can't just decide to earn £2,500 per month – that is not enough detail to be sure that you can really focus on what you need to be doing. So let's break that down into how you spend your time.

I believe we can use four categories (I love it when things are in fours – it's neat and geometrical). They are as follows:

1. Income generating time – time that you can actually send someone an invoice for.
2. Income speculating time – time spent networking for a client or speaking with a live and interested vendor.
3. Income saving time – time spent on accounts and property maintenance. It is just as important to keep your money once you have it as it is to acquire it in the first place.
4. Other – this includes everything from personal development, family and fitness, to reading a book, or anything you want to do that does not fall into the first three core categories – life!

How do you spend your time?

Saves Money

Admin | Income generation

Not Invoicable | **Invoicable**

Other* | Income speculation

Costs Money

Other – non-business activities, e.g. personal development, sports, hobbies, socialising.

Again, you can keep a record over a month and see how you spend your time. Right now, by writing this book, I am spending a lot of time on income speculating activity. This is because, although I will sell this book in the future (you are reading it after all), I cannot send an invoice to anyone while I am writing it.

How you spend your time is very relevant to your cashflow position because if you are expenses-high and income-poor, then you have to spend more time generating income than anything else. If you are at equilibrium (where income equals expenses), then you can think about growing your business to the next level – to generate more income – and so spend some time on income speculation activities.

How much does an hour cost?

The next step is to calculate your hourly rate. Given that you will spend only a portion of your time actually invoicing for income, you can imagine that you will not have an hourly rate in the same way an employee has one (based on just showing up at their place of work) – that simply is not enough now!

Let's say that out of the 52 weeks of the year you will work for 48 weeks – you will need time off to recharge your batteries, see family and have the odd bank holiday. If you are still in a very active learning phase and part of a programme around property, personal development or on a mentorship, you will need to add in time to allow you to complete these activities too.

Now out of the 48 weeks (roughly 11 months) you will not work weekends (in an ideal world – of course in reality you might) and you will aim to work Monday to Friday for about eight hours per day (nine to five). You can reduce this if you are planning to work part time.

So, depending on what you offer to clients, in whatever form that takes, you will have chargeable time. In my case (so you can see how this works), let's say in one week I could source a property for a client, offer a three-hour strategy session and also coach people one-to-one or teach them in a group.

Next let's think about how much time I can invoice for. This is looking at it in one direction – we will come back and check feasibility in a minute. Well, I estimate I can source one property a week, have one strategy session and then five coaching clients. Okay, how many hours will that take?

- Sourcing a property from start to finish = 8 days
- Strategy session = 3 hours
- Mentoring = 5 x 1 hour

Well, the above clearly doesn't work as the total comes to more hours than there are in a week – nine days in fact. That's two more days than available on any of the calendars I know.

Let's be more realistic and reverse the process. Let's estimate one property to be sourced per month (eight days), one strategy session per month (three hours) and one coaching client per month (four hours). So that is a rough total of nine invoice days per month.

Now my target earnings were £30,000 per year and I have 11 months of working time – so that is £2,727 per month. When divided by my nine potential invoice days, that gives a daily rate of £303 per day. If I can invoice for seven hours per day, then I could charge £43.28 per hour.

The reality of this exercise is that you will need more than £30,000 to cover the expenses of running your business. You will need to pay for travel, marketing, advertising, membership to certain professional bodies and certain training courses – you will also need a mentor.

The £30,000 will need to be **net income after expenses deducted** from your business turnover. Depending on what services you offer clients, how you find them and distances you have to travel, then you will have to double or even triple the £30,000 target to generate that level of profit. So, in reality, your daily rate to earn £30,000 per year needs to be approximately £80–£130 per hour if you are only going to invoice nine days a month. You could, of course, work more days a month…

You can start to see that you can move these figures around. Let's say you want a turnover of £90,000 to give at least £30,000 clear profit.

£90,000 / 11 months = £8,182 per month (approximately).

Let's say you invoice for 10 days per month. This means you need to charge £818 per day. So, if it takes ten days work to identify, source, manage and tenant a property for a client, then you need to charge a minimum of £8,180 plus travel if you source long distance. This will also mean that you have to charge VAT!

Do it at home – do it at work

As with your household, you will need to monitor the business expenses as well as the business income. In the first year or two it will cost more, as you may set up a website, or make mistakes on advertising or in other areas. You may also have a higher learning cost as a percentage than in later years.

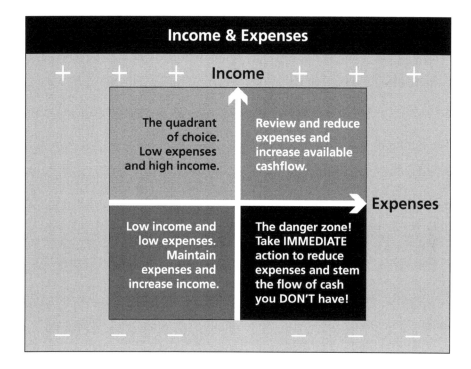

Income & Expenses

Income

The quadrant of choice. Low expenses and high income.	Review and reduce expenses and increase available cashflow.
Low income and low expenses. Maintain expenses and increase income.	The danger zone! Take IMMEDIATE action to reduce expenses and stem the flow of cash you DON'T have!

Expenses

I hope this helps you to understand the following three key concepts:

1. Know what is happening with your income and expenses – track them and make corrections so that you get back to at least equilibrium as soon as possible.
2. Know what you need to earn a year to calculate your hourly rate – remember to cover the business expenses as well as the household expenses.
3. Make sure your strategy pays. Go back and look at how much time you spend to get a cashflowing deal and work out your hourly rate. If it takes a year to get one deal at £200 per month, then 200 x 12 is £2,400 per annum. If you are working 11 months, 20 days per month, seven hours a day, then your hourly rate will be £1.56!

The game of consequences

I remember hearing the phrase: 'Every decision has a consequence – evaluate the consequences upfront!' and I love it. Sometimes we make rash decisions and they work out, other times they don't. Sometimes we don't make a decision and nothing changes. Sometimes everything goes wrong. Personally, I prefer to make decisions, take action and influence the shape of my life.

I have had a few philosophical debates over recent months about people believing their life is preordained and therefore they don't need to worry as 'what will be will be'. I don't think it is a question of preordained, predetermined or self-created – the question is one of involvement and participation. There is a joke:

A man found himself the sole survivor of a shipwreck and as he prayed to God in the water he asked to be saved: 'Please God save me.' A little while later, a large piece of wreckage passed by floating on the surface and the man ignored it as he continued to pray: 'Please God save me.' After an hour, a boat passed by and he ignored it and continued to pray: 'Please God save me.' As the day grew on and the man grew weary, a plane flew over the site of the boat's last-known sighting; it circled and left as the man continued to pray: 'Please God save me.' Finally, exhausted, the man could no longer tread water and drowned. As he arrived at the gates of Heaven, the man asked St Peter, 'What happened? I prayed and prayed to be saved. Why didn't God save me?' St Peter said, 'He sent a piece of wreckage, a boat and a plane – what more did you want?'

The point I hope I have made is, no matter what your beliefs are, you need to play your role in your life to achieve the outcomes you want, or are destined to have. What choices or decisions are you making and have you evaluated them?

Consequences

- If you give up work or don't manage your credit score, you will not be able to get a mortgage in your own name.

- If you don't understand the value of your time and the time cost of your chosen strategy, you will run out of money as your expenses exceed your income.

- If you don't have a clear strategy of how to make money from your property knowledge, you will not create the cashflow you need to sustain your lifestyle, even as it is now.

- If you are not clear about your focus, you will flit from one strategy to another and from one deal to another until you fail.

- If you don't know why you want to do this or what you expect from property, then what will keep you going when you face the challenges we all must face? Why will you succeed when others fail? What will make you successful?

What are the consequences of the decisions you are making (or not making)?

- On-going debt.
- Increasing debt.
- No mortgages.
- No cashflowing deals.
- No income.
- No success.
- Failure, disappointment and resignation as you return to a job to make ends meet in a worse situation than when you left work.

So the actions you need to take now are simple:

- First, record and monitor your time and work out how much time certain key activities take you.

- Second, monitor your expenses – understand if you are income-rich or expenses-poor.

This will give you the outline of your personal financial strategy:

- You will understand whether or not you can 'afford' to follow a certain investment strategy.

- You will be able to take immediate and decisive action to ensure that your finances are at least at a point of equilibrium.

- You can make informed decisions about the 'services' you can offer and what they will cost.

- You know how much your time is worth and can choose to spend it differently – is four hours in front of the TV worth the lost £400 of potential income you could have earned?

Moving on to the money

Section 1 covers the critical skills that I recognised in other successful entrepreneurs and decided to discover, develop or enhance for my own purpose, to become independently wealthy and financially free.

Why reinvent the wheel? If you see people achieving the goals and business success you want, then work out what it is that they know and understand that you don't. Then learn and understand it for yourself.

I started with this type of knowledge as I believe that all successful and long-lasting business people have developed the skills to master their own minds before they start mastering money. That's the difference between a wealthy future and a lottery winner lifestyle. Successful people understand that self-belief, focus and action get results.

Now that your mind is mastered and you understand 'why' you want to invest in property and have a property business, rather than just remain an investor, it's time to move on to mastering the money. Understanding the financial markets and how money flows is critical in business and even more so in property investment. Successful people understand that it is the relative value of money and the skill in leveraging that money that creates long-lasting wealth.

SECTION 2

Understanding the
economic environment

Chapter 4

The business of investing

You need to shift your thinking from an investor mindset (looking for houses and cash) to a business mindset – a more entrepreneurial way of thinking. When you start to think about serving markets, consumer needs and supply and demand, the result will be a shift in business growth.

- Do you understand the tax, mindset and business benefits of being an investor or business owner rather than an employee?

- Have you thought how Brexit will impact on the British housing market?

- Have you considered the impact of Section 24 – tax relief limited to 20% on mortgage interest – on your business model and portfolio and on that of your potential clients and other landlords?

- Do you think of money as real money, or recognise its relative worth and leverage potential?

This chapter will take you through the fundamental economic lessons I have picked up – in a simple-to-understand way:

- Seize opportunities to become financially free.

- Education – where to look.

- Strategy – how to pick the right one.

- Leverage other people's money.

- What's your offer?

- Do you know your value?

- Have you got the right team and can you lead them?

Nothing is the same: B and I > E and S

Whether you have given up work or plan to, have savings and equity to invest or are borrowing money, you must protect your financial future by understanding what is going on in the market and how it *will* affect you. Anything else and you really are gambling with your future, and that is definitely *not* what I am about.

This book is all about changing your mindset and business model from investor to business owner. In the previous chapters, I have discussed the mental skills and concepts I believe are vital to success. What I haven't done yet, is explain why and how to make that step change to become a business owner.

With changes being introduced under Section 24 – the reduction of mortgage interest tax relief to a basic 20% – there is a lot of discussion about setting up limited companies. The actual decision needs to be personal and based on specific tax advice about your costs and benefits.

The key to understand the change is this – if you keep your current earnings below the 40% tax threshold then you will not be affected. Attributing certain allowable expenses to your business can reduce household expenses. Learning to think like a business owner will have wider benefits as well.

You need to understand the principals of tax as they affect you and your investments.

Employee		Business owner or investor	
Earns	£1,000	Earns	£1,000
Tax @ 35% including National Insurance	-£350	Expenses including phone, travel and internet	-£270
Take home pay	£650	Profit liable for tax	£730
Cost of phone, travel and internet	-£270	Tax @ 35%	-£255.50
What's left?	£380	What's left?	£474.50

Depending on the business model, expenses could be considerably higher.

Tax benefits are just one reason to think like a business owner. I believe the real benefit of being a business owner is the acknowledgement that you are taking active responsibility for your financial future and all that entails.

Remember, I explained that every decision has a consequence. Just evaluate it upfront. If this section or topic is stressful, perhaps because you feel you don't understand it, then learn it. Without being rude, it is that simple. I sat in a class at school where the teacher spoke about economics and I stared out of the window! Now I know how vital it is – a core business skill that you need to learn and keep updated. It can be as simple as reading the *Financial Times*, the business and financial sections of *The Times* or *The Guardian*, checking the BBC or Sky News websites for stories – or change who you talk to – who you listen to.

Go where the conversations are happening! What events do you go to? Are they just property related? Do you network with business owners outside the property sphere? What about the Business Show in 2017 or 2018 are you going – they happen twice a year? If not, why not? You need to know this stuff.

My economic and business mentors

Apart from the greats, like Sir Richard Branson and Lord Alan Sugar, there are other reliable and easily accessible sources of forward-thinking economic and business knowledge and one is Robert Kiyosaki, author of *Rich Dad Poor Dad* (1997) and, another interesting author is Tony Robbins *Unshakeable: Your Guide to Financial Freedom* (2017) even the *Financial Times* has a guide!

Opportunities to hear people like Branson, Sugar and Kiyosaki speak are possible but rare. There are a great many other brilliant thinkers and speakers about business, money flows and the economy; if you get an opportunity, go along and listen. Through my connection with Ecademy and Daniel Priestley, founder of Triumphant Events, I have been fortunate enough to hear Nic Rixon speak about his attitude to business, money, the economy and much more.

As you join certain mailing lists you will come across a diverse range of events and opportunities to hear fascinating people speak. Go. Remember your objective is to learn not to fall into a hard sales trap, but to listen with purpose and identify your knowledge gaps. Then leave and make a plan – identify what is your next most critical action, as opposed to the next course to go on. Some key lessons I have gathered include:

- focus in the form of sticking to one business idea and pursuing it to success

- economic lifecycle – not in terms of boom and bust, but in terms of business era – defining business drive, what are the current economic motivators

- intention – or, as I would say, 'Why?' What is your passion?

- money – how we use it over family generations – what it means to us, and how to leverage it.

Initially, Kiyosaki has dramatically influenced the direction of my financial understanding and my wider financial plans due to reading (and listening to) his books. He was the first step on my financial education. All too often the books are written by Americans and talk of 401Ks (their pensions) which can be complicated. Find a European writer or even better a British financial expert you get along with. See my bibliography at the back of the book.

- Know the difference between assets and liabilities.

- Understand how money flows.

- Don't put all of your faith in the government or education system – they want you to have a job and pay taxes.

- Get a financial education so you understand money.

Lord Alan Sugar understands the core fundamentals of business – how to buy, sell, market and invest. Above all, his mind bending, and life refocusing question is, 'Where is the money? If the business is not going to make money in the first few months, it's not a business.'

Sir Richard Branson inspires everyone to 'follow your heart, find your passion, make a difference' and 'just do it'. Behind all the passion and media attention is an incredible businessman who, like Lord Alan Sugar, inspires and leads a fantastic team of business brains without whose support none of his success would be possible.

Who are the new thought leaders? Do you know who Gary Vaynerchuk is? What has James Dyson or Elon Musk got planned? Where will new British business champions emerge and what does that mean for local economies? Equally, where will changes occur that will have less positive impacts? Victoria Beckham is ranked more highly than Lord Alan Sugar on the UK 100 Entrepreneur list 2016! Do you know what she does?

Do you know who Michael Acton Smith is? As the founder of Calm.com and Mind Candy he created Moshi Monsters and World of Warriors. I have wandered into another world and another language here, but there are lessons to be learnt. New technologies beget new business opportunities and new ways of learning!

I am going to cover in brief a few of these economic lessons. You may start to see a pattern and almost a repetition as these messages come from so many different sources. So, let's start by putting these overlapping lessons in some form of order – not out of preference or importance, just for the sake of structure.

Focus and intention

The message here seems to be the usual – focus on one thing until successful and then you can diversify. The underlying point is that there is a time lag (and a series of skills) needed to be successful in a chosen field. Too many small businesses bump along just making ends meet, as they repeatedly switch business focus – for example, property to stocks, or investing to rent-to-rent to the internet! Within any field of business be clear – become an expert and let your clients and market know who and what you stand for.

This is where I use the word 'why?' others use words like intention, purpose or passion. We often know 'why' we want to do something or what we want our business to result in; we know what our intention is by starting a business venture.

If you can't articulate 'why' at the moment, then make it a priority to draw this out and develop it. It is not a static thing. It is okay to evolve your future the more you experience, the more you can imagine. Tom Evans, a great friend and mentor of mine, comments that you will be stifled by the limitations of what you can imagine now – whereas your thoughts can be expanded by imagining what you could learn.

The business message here is: start your business idea with the end in mind. How much do you want to earn? What do you want to do? What do you want to have? How do you want to work on a day-to-day basis? What is your exit strategy? What will you have created? What will you leave behind?

Economic lifecycle

This is fascinating and I am sure common knowledge to some people. This is not the usual economic cycle of boom and bust, or even the interesting perspective of the baby boomers, their children and the impact of their associated spending habits as they pass through the economic cycle.

This is about the 'eras of business' – the developments and fundamental shifts in corporate thinking.

For example:

- 1950s–60s was the production era – a bubble of innovation and productivity in post-war England. Then, as we hit the late 1960s, it was hard to differentiate one product from another, so

- 1970s–80s became the image marketing era – remember the Marlborough Man?

- By 1990, the world was swamped with images. Now we needed companies to position themselves, place themselves in the mind of the client with a message that said why they were different. We became more time conscious and looked for the perfect pitch that spoke directly to us and our individual needs.

- In 2000, the web became more mainstream and companies identified it as a new marketing channel, and so it became the distribution era.

Small businesses tend to follow these trend about 10 years behind that of large corporate shifts. This means that 2010 onwards is the dawn of the distribution era for small businesses as more than 50% of sales move to the web. While small businesses are focused on developing online sales, the corporates have moved back round the cycle to production, as they need new products that just use the online medium, for example, Kindle and iPhones.

There is an overlying impact that human generational-spending (my word) has had and continues to have on the economy. The culture, buying and spending habits of each generation impact on the economy and how the money flows. For example, a generation of spenders takes money from wages and spends it in the economy; a generation of savers puts their money in the bank rather than directly into circulation.

The bulges of population caused by the baby boomers and now their children are sweeping through the economy, as a large percentage of the population all reach an age of consumer demand at the same time – they all have children so sales in baby-related products soar. The children of the baby boomer generation are starting to leave home with the impact that family homes are now too big for their needs. The baby boomers spend on their children until they leave home and then all their focus shifts to their savings. They are starting to downsize towards retirement.

The younger generation are leaving university with mountains of debt and need to move out into the real world away from parents. Mostly, they will have to move into the rental market as the combination of debt and lack of savings means they do not have the means to buy their own home. As they start to join the employment market there could be a rise in their disposable income. This spending bulge will arrive as their parents reduce their spending in response to forthcoming retirement. The popularity of consumable products will swing from those items attractive to the 50+ age group to those favoured by educated and technologically aware 20-somethings.

What if you could get ahead of the small business curve by emulating big business? What could you do to increase your business through the product concept? I know you are a property investor but you still need to understand the web and, more importantly, social media. Credibility and your investor or client's ability to check you out online has never been more important. What happens if I Google you? Do you appear professional or do you appear to be someone who is not serious about business?

There has to be a reason to go digital – you need a business purpose. There is no point 'tweeting' to thousands of people if you cannot convert those conversations to sales. That is why property businesses will have products and services to sell to clients at all levels of the sales chain; from high-value face-to-face services through to lower-cost replicable products or services.

What do you need to learn? Who do you need to talk with to understand the digital medium as a communication channel and maximise your opportunity to transact business through the web? What do you need to do to enhance your credibility along with your sales?

Get a financial education – asset, liabilities and cashflow

We all went to school, theoretically, to get a good education. In fact, we were trained. The term 'education' comes from the Latin meaning to 'pull out' or 'draw out'. Do you feel that your internal knowledge was pulled out, that it flowed from you? Or did you sit there and recite the alphabet and times table, like me?

I have written earlier in the Introduction to this book about the difference between education, understanding and training – it is the difference between having the information but not the knowledge and understanding to apply it. Take algebra as a case in point.

The British education system does not prepare young people, I would argue, for life or the world of work. Young people are not taught about assets and liabilities, about income and expenses. They might, depending on their choices at A Level, do some basic accounts as part of a business course, but there is no context or linking back to the real lives ahead of them. Why? Because the system needs them to be employees!

If you have children, the greatest gifts you can give them are, first, the game of Monopoly, then move on to CashFlow for Kids. They were, after all, born to keep you in the style you would like your old age to be – luxurious. So you'd better give them the education to manage their money and invest it wisely in property and not the building society or designer clothes!

Money – how it flows, is used and is leveraged

Earlier, I covered leverage and ROI in a lot of detail; understanding these concepts is vital for success. If you do not understand how money moves and what it costs, how can you access it and afford to pay to borrow it?

Shirlaw talks about the concepts of 'relative money' and 'real money'. The poor think about and deal with real money – that is the pound coins and five pound notes in their wallets. They try to acquire it and then they want to hold on to it. They do not understand the relative value of money. They don't understand the power and value of leverage.

The rich and super rich understand about the relative value of money and you do too! Money is a resource that can be used and leveraged to create more money. Understanding money is a continuum: at one end, people with no idea and no money; at the other end, people grasping and holding tightly to the small amounts they do possess, in fear of losing what they have. If you recognise money as a resource to be used, then you reside in the middle with the rich and super wealthy.

What are your thoughts about money?

Underlying this understanding about money is the concept of abundance. This can apply to so many areas of your life. I know without a shadow of a doubt

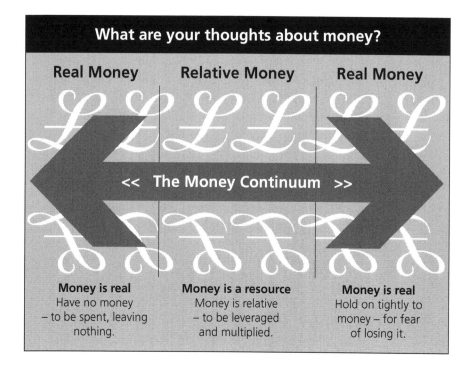

What are your thoughts about money?

Real Money **Relative Money** **Real Money**

<< The Money Continuum >>

Money is real	**Money is a resource**	**Money is real**
Have no money – to be spent, leaving nothing.	Money is relative – to be leveraged and multiplied.	Hold on tightly to money – for fear of losing it.

that you are one of the top 10% richest people in the world – simply because you are reading this book. Do you feel abundant? It depends what you use as a comparison, of course. The truth is you are rich in so many ways – revel in that feeling for a while.

Let's think about water. Is water abundant? You know where to find it and how to gather it when you need to use it, mostly because we are spoilt by taps and bottled mineral water. Yet, if you were about to cross the desert, would you learn even more about water – that precious life-preserving resource? That is what money is – a precious resource. You need to learn about where to find it and how and when to use it.

To explain leveraging a business and business capacity, consider the metaphor of a glass and its contents – water. If the glass is full (either your head with knowledge and ideas or your business with sales), then you cannot grow until you tip out some of the water to let more flow in or get a bigger glass. Let's get a bigger glass and pour all the water (or business) from the first glass into the larger second glass. What happens is that you have more space in the second glass to add more water (business sales or knowledge).

In this model, the crucial figures are between 40–80% capacity. If your business sales and cashflow reside between these figures, great, as long as that is enough cash to meet the life of your dreams. If your business for whatever reason is producing less than 40% of your potential sales income or using less than 40% of your total sales opportunity time, then you will have a lower cashflow, and even cashflow issues.

Alternatively, if your business is operating at 80% capacity or above, then I guarantee you are stressed. You need to develop systems, outsource and/or grow your business. You need to expand your business into a bigger model or a larger glass.

I mentioned valuing your time and working out what you are worth in Chapter 3 on page 51. I said that you had four ways of using your time: income generating; income speculating; income saving; and 'other'. If you now apply this level of understanding to the concept above, you need to make sure that your business invoices or generates income for 80% of the month – that means 24 days.

Remember the example I showed when we were calculating your hourly rate? If you only work (invoice and earn money) for 10 days a month, then you are only working at 30% capacity. Why? Because you could be earning money for 30 days per month if you developed the systems, products and services to meet your client's needs. If you invoiced £800 a day for 365 days a year, that would be £292,000 before costs and tax. If you get the systems right that is not going to be the same as 'working' for 365 days of your life!

How is this possible if you have to spend time speculating, saving and living your life? Because you outsource the capacity and that is how your business grows. An easy example is to use a letting agent – trade 10% of your rent for their time. They will manage the property, the tenant and the repairs and you use the time to source more properties and generate more income. Another example is to use trades people to refurbish your property rather than doing it yourself. They are quicker (guaranteed because they do it all the time), more professional (ditto) and your time is more valuably spent sourcing other deals.

Leadership

So this brings us to leadership and the examples set by Lord Alan Sugar and Sir Richard Branson. They have different styles that we may never truly understand until we experience it personally, but what they have in common is a clear vision – expertly communicated to all of their staff. Both are passionate men – they just have different styles and personalities. Sugar and Branson understand the vision and purpose of their businesses, communicating them clearly to the staff team and encouraging their buy-in, support and contribution. These have to be traits of leadership.

How to apply this and become a business owner

Instead of being a property investor who buys houses and gets stuck when there is no more money, I believe that if you think like and become a property business owner with all the concepts talked about so far, then you will grow your business and your portfolio quicker and more easily than many others. You'll also pay less tax in the process!

There are two selling points for me:

1. You can start thinking in terms of products and services and that is more creative than just houses.
2. You can start to leverage your time, money and, more importantly, other people's time and money, and all by taking active responsibility.

Think about products and services for a minute – how is this different from thinking about houses? I recognised that my tenant was actually a customer who I was selling to. I was selling them the idea that they wanted to live in my property and that they wanted to stay there for a long time. Then I thought about the vendor – what service could I offer them? Then my estate agent, and so on. It has changed the way I do business and has opened up lots of opportunities that I have put into practice.

I also thought about what I had to offer – what do people who I meet want from me? I soon realised that people wanted to know how I started and what I had been doing. So I wrote a book. I saw the book as a way to use my time effectively – write once, share many times. Then I had my first product and my first marketing tool.

This time, I have written a book using a more professional, cost- and time-effective system. This book will generate more profit than the first edition because I have employed a great team, the strategy was planned from the start and the marketing is better – I recognise this is a product. The third book will do even better as I apply the new lessons I am learning, and so on.

Finally, in 2011, I took the very challenging step (for me as a committed control freak) to outsource some of my business. Even as I write, I can think of more tasks that I want to hand over to my virtual team. I understand that virtual staff can be sourced on the web – there are plenty of sites depending on what skills you need. However, I preferred to meet and get to know the person who was going to work with me – so I used Skype as a way to 'see' them and learn to trust them – old fashioned and unnecessary and something that definitely slowed me down. Having said this, I know plenty of investors who are landlords because they don't trust a letting agent! We now have a replicable system that other investors can follow – complete with 'how to' and 'what if' instructions – another new product.

So, why be a business owner? Because you can leverage other people's time and money to grow your property portfolio quicker and more easily. *Why do that?* So that you can be financially secure and start enjoying the financial freedom and lifestyle that you want.

Is this compelling enough?

How do you become a business owner?

You need to take this knowledge and understanding and apply it to your own circumstances. You need to decide on your own repeatable and replicable model of property sourcing. You need to identify where your skills and experience lie, what your knowledge and passion is about. This will form the basis of your business model.

So just to repeat the steps:

1. Know why you want to invest in property. What do you expect to get out of it? What will the business look like? How much will you earn (do the maths)? How will you earn your cashflow?
2. Get financially educated; you have started by reading this book, now look at who you mix with – what groups you attend. Expand your network. Join non-property groups but choose those that do not burden you with building other people's businesses. Have conversations with your accountant, tax advisor and other business owners. Get a good broker who follows the market and can discuss the mood of the Monetary Policy Committee with you. Who can you connect with, talk to and listen to about all things financial and economic?
3. Pick the right strategy and know the other strategies that can be used if necessary. Remember about the value of your time – make sure the strategy will pay you a decent 'wage' for your time, otherwise Tesco, Marks & Spencer or Boots is starting to look like a better option! Understand what you want to achieve financially and then give yourself the best possible chance of achieving it. My money 'is on' and comes from property sourcing. I am my own client and so my system is replicable. It is costed to make sure I earn a decent amount for my time (which is a valuable and limited resource – the only limited resource in reality!)
4. Leverage where possible – use other people's money and other people's time. You will need to understand the relative cost of money and ROI in order to explain the opportunity to potential clients. Outsource by using a letting agent, bookkeeper, accountant, builder and, if you can, a cleaner. Work these costings into your business model.

5. Understand what you have to offer your clients. What is your service? Why should they sell to you or buy or rent from you and not someone else? To do this you will need to understand what you know, what you have experience of, what your skills are and where your passion lies. It is one of the fundamental bits of personal analysis that we do with mentees, because if you can't explain to me why I should do business with you, then I will work with someone else who can. Then remember in this seemingly 'me-me' world that what you have to offer has to be all about 'them' and not about 'you'. To make that transition from understanding yourself to understanding your client market is crucial; so crucial that the success of your business will rest upon you achieving it. Know your client, picture them, know where to find them and always speak directly to them. Refine it over time – it will change. It has to be good, but it does not have to be perfect first time! Develop your niche and message accordingly.

6. Know your value. What are you selling and what is it worth? Recognise whether you are selling a replicable model (what you do) or the skills to act as an agent (not location or strategy specific).

7. Get the right team. I have already mentioned that you need to speak to the right people to increase your financial knowledge; you also need the right team to deliver a service to your clients. Know that you can trust the people you are building your business around. You don't need to use just one solicitor or even just one broker. A level of consistency will build trust and relationships, but you need to be prepared to change if their ability to meet your service needs doesn't come up to your expected standard or response times. Just a word of caution here – if you are only passing on one deal a quarter, you are probably not a top client – so build on your business and that relationship first.

Section 3 explains the practicalities and specifics of setting up a sourcing business.

Continuous professional development and accountability

Continuing your training is crucial, but there is a balance to be had. In the early days of your investing career you will find yourself attending four to six property networks a month or more. Soon you will recognise that you want a personal life. That you are tired of being sold to, of wasting evenings learning nothing of value. You will become more discerning about where you spend your time and your money.

By going to fewer events, you will have more time to think about what you wanted to get out of each event that you do attend. What was my intention for attending? If you can clearly articulate what you want to learn, then you can seek out the right teachers, mentors and coaches. If you can clearly articulate who you want to meet, then you can attend the right events and networks.

When it comes to coaching I have the following approach; I have taken on a variety of business or skill-specific coaches for a period of time to acquire certain knowledge. For example, I spent time enhancing my sales skills, mastering website strategies, developing my books and other products, and business and product development, and so on. Decide where in your business you need help and then find the person most skilled.

So what if I just want to be a property investor?

Great, that's a brilliant choice because at least you have read the previous chapters in this book. You have had a chance to see the opportunity and decided that it is not right for you at this moment, unless of course you have an underlying negative belief.

What difference will it make? Maybe none. If you have found a system that works and you have all the cashflow that you need, plus the time to enjoy it, then it is a brilliant choice.

I suspect, if you are reading this book, it is because you want something more – you are searching for ideas on how to do something better.

Case study – retire as early as you want

I have been working with a client for the last six months, learning what she wants from life, her attitude towards risk and her financial situation. It all boiled down to a desire to retire early, to get away from the well-placed corporate job that was stopping her from having even more of the life she wanted. The biggest challenge was breaking through the traditional thinking that she had learned from parents, schools and other people she worked with. Gradually, I answered her questions and demonstrated that there was another way. I provided the evidence ROI. More importantly, she was able to check this out, independently, with her financial advisor. What more could you ask for than third-party endorsement?

The client owned a relatively mortgage-free property and, like a lot of people she also had a significant sum of cash she could access.

We had strategy session and I demonstrated how cashflowing investments could provide the first level of financial security she craved. I showed her the examples of recent deals I had done for other clients.

This initial portfolio would also become the foundation to her larger deals as lenders would see her as a professional investor and therefore apply different lending criteria.

As much as she wanted, we could not get corporate HMO finance for a new investor with no experience. She had to wait. She now has a reasonable portfolio cashflowing £3,500 per month and is in the position to move on to larger deals.

Chapter 5

Money – the reality

When you understand how the money market works and what lenders want, then all excuses to succeed fly out of the window. I will explain what various lenders want from their borrowers and how and where to get your information. There are risks and consequences and it is not all about having the 'right' state of mind, although that definitely helps!

Using credit cards to buy a property or fund a project

Like all lending, the most important thing before you start is to understand how much it is going to cost you to borrow the money, when you can pay it back and who is going to pay the interest in the meantime.

However, in its simplest form, a credit card if used properly can give you up to 45 days extra money – interest free. In its most strategic form, it can lend you most of the deposit or costs for an investment project at 0% interest for between 9 and 15 months! Your challenge, with everything associated to borrowing money, is to understand the money flow of your deal. When you will pay it back, where that money will come from, and who is going to pay the interest on the money while the project is being worked.

The next challenge is how to borrow money on a credit card without affecting your credit score. Please be aware that lenders share information behind the scenes as they are all owned by one massive shareholder – us, through the government. This means that even a last-minute application for a credit card, right before completion, could result in your mortgage offer being pulled – beware!

Money management system – stuff they really don't want you to know

Banks want you to stay ignorant of the game and how it works. On one hand, they want you to take out credit cards and buy stuff that really you can't afford, so that at the end of the month you can't clear your credit card balance and instead pay them an extortionate rate of interest. On the other hand, they now also want you to be a perfect borrower. From a secured lending perspective, the underwriters of mortgages need you to demonstrate that you know how to manage your money. The way that you can do this is to limit the amount of unsecured borrowing (credit cards) that you have available, clear your balances regularly, yet keep borrowing and paying back.

Now the experts out there will be telling you to apply for credit cards, because you need to show you can manage your money and also, if you have access to credit on cards, then you can buy their expensive courses. What you must understand is how a lender views the activity on your credit record and how this affects your credit score and, ultimately, your ability to borrow money through mortgages.

First, do not apply for too many credit cards at once or apply to have your existing cards increase their limits. Just by asking, you are affecting your credit score whether or not you are successful. Second, when you have cards, do not 'max them out' and use every last pound available to you, as you will look out of control and desperate for cash. Have a strategy to pay back your cards regularly and even overpay them now and then.

I am not going to go into any more detail about credit cards here as my first book, *Using Other People's Money*, covers this extensively. Suffice to say, credit cards are a brilliant tool if you know how to use them.

What is gearing?

Gearing is a measure that a lender uses to measure how much you have actually borrowed, particularly on unsecured lending like credit cards, against how much available credit you have. You need to get to a position where you are borrowing under 50% of your potential borrowing, ie. have a gearing ratio of less than 50%. How do you work this out? Add up the total debt on all your credit cards and divide it by the total of all your credit limits.

I have guessed the figure of 50%. When I first increased my credit cards to cover my training costs, my credit rating dropped through the floor. I called the credit agencies and spoke with them – they can be very helpful. They explained about gearing and I started to experiment by paying off my 0% credit cards bit by bit as they came to the end of the life of the offers. I noticed that my credit rating started to improve as my gearing ratio moved towards 60%. Of course, other factors will have been at play – like the number of searches on my record, but I do believe gearing is now a significant decision-making factor.

Summary – good habits for managing your credit cards effectively

1. Get your credit reports and credit scores regularly – at least every other month – and check your information.
2. Minimise the number of applications you make to a maximum of one every other month and fewer than three in six months.
3. Don't reapply if you have just been turned down – wait until you get your credit reports, repair the problem and then wait again before continuing.
4. *Always* set up a direct debit payment and then overpay the minimum payment each month as you see fit.
5. Keep a spreadsheet and track each card, know your credit limit, know when you last asked for an increase, know when your 0% deal runs out and clear that card first.
6. Aim to bring your gearing ratio down by making focused payments.
7. Clear any cards that are accruing interest charges as a priority.
8. Remember, good debt is for purchases that earn you money (for example, a property purchase or refurbishment) and bad debt is the purchase of goods or services that reduce in value and cost you money.
9. Know how you will get the money back out of a deal to repay your cards and, if appropriate, who is paying the interest.

Playing the lenders at their own game

When I was in my poor phase as a single mother, literally counting every single 10 pence piece I spent, the credit card was my saviour. I put my university grant money in a high-rate deposit account and I made every purchase I could by credit card – while still knowing my budget and my income. I then cleared the credit card every month, in full, from the savings account – one withdrawal. At the end of the year, the bank gave me approximately £100 interest for managing my money, which the girls and I spent on our summer holidays and having fun.

It might not seem like a lot, but it was a great return (roughly 3–4% better than the building society) for relatively little effort, during a time when my budget for food and entertainment was very limited!

I later developed this skill and learned how to play the 0% off-set game. To work this strategy, you need an off-set or 'One' mortgage account. Then you borrow money at 0% from your credit card and deposit it into your off-set mortgage account. This effectively discounts your mortgage by the amount borrowed at 0% on your credit card. It's brilliant in today's market where it is better to off-set your mortgage as mortgage interest is 3–6% and savings interest only 1–2%. These accounts can then also become a personal source of pre-authorised lending and practically free borrowing.

Listen to the market experts

I knew nothing about this before I started to invest. I soon realised that if I wanted to borrow money in a challenging market, then I needed to understand what the people who were going to lend me money wanted from me. How did I find the information? By seeking out conversations with experts who know about the economy. Do you belong to the NLA (National Landlord Association)? What about the RLA (Residential Landlords Association)? Go to the Property Shows and listen to the money people not just the investors and course sellers.

Listen to speakers at events – repeatedly ask people in the property industry what they think about the market and start to form an opinion. I keep getting newsletters saying that interest rates will go up – well, yes, of course they will, but not in the next month (at the time of writing this of course). How do I know this? If you check the Bank of England's monthly meeting reports where they discuss interest rates, you'll see that only one person wants rates to be increased! As that mood and number of votes change, then there is a real risk of immediate interest rates increasing. With inflation driven by energy prices rather than consumer spending, any increase in interest rates will not slow borrowing and inflation; it will kill any potential growth in high-street sales. With Brexit on the horizon the government's focus is on growth and that comes through consumer spending.

Risk and consequences

Having said this, you need to 'stress-test' all loans. What if interest rates go up by, let's say, 5%? What would your net monthly cashflow be? If less than £100, then maybe you need to rethink if the deal has enough cashflow to stand changes in the market – or maybe consider a 3–5-year fixed rate loan (subject to strategy of course). You will be lucky to get a loan that has not already been seriously stressed tested, but don't assume – do your own sums!

Rates will go up. 'When?' is an educated question and subject to so many external factors that it is almost impossible to tell. Whatever happens, you need to be prepared! Know the risks and consequences of the debt you are taking on.

Whatever strategy you decide and whatever amount of effort you put in to understand the money markets and economics, it is up to you. I would suggest that the more proactively responsible you are, the more you mitigate the risk of investing. The only one who can protect your family and your financial future and dreams is you! No blame, just responsibility, and with that comes more control and a refined decision-making ability.

A very brief history – banking and the money markets

During 2008 and 2009, the availability of money in the marketplace and high street was, as we know, severely constricted, as banks and mortgage lenders pulled out of the lending market, either through poor performance or simply the lack of trust and the resultant short supply of funds available to lend. They stayed out until mid to late 2011.

During the next 3–4 years, the market settled until the Mortgage Market Review 2014 focused in on the residential mortgage loan market and the concept of 'affordability'. In 2016/17, attention turned towards the buy-to-let lending market. These changes have come on top of tax changes and an increased shift towards corporate (limited company) lending. This means the mortgage market is currently evolving to meet new demands from consumers and from legislation. A broker will be able to advise you on current opportunities and restrictions.

I believe we need to understand how 'money works' so that when we approach our lenders to see whether we can borrow money from them to invest in property, we understand their business – what they need from an ideal client, like us. Moving to more commercial lending means having conversations as a business client of the bank, which entails a whole different language.

What does the future hold? More of the same! No matter what Europe proposes in terms of regulation and post-Brexit 'punishments', or America with its powerfully placed advocates of 'us first' (and consequences be damned), they are unlikely to agree to a globally acceptable business finance strategy or a sensible approach towards risk.

And there are other emerging global players focused on their own growth and wealth. How will they fit in – or make their marks? What will that mean to the British economy as changes ripple through?

I believe we need to start the money moving at the bottom of the food chain again. We need to get spending personally and commercially, in a responsible and calculated way to promote business and commerce. We need to go round the outside of these major banks and investment houses to the private individuals with money. These people have also been failed by a system designed to support the 'uber-rich' on a scale that we cannot even comprehend. Know what you have to offer, know what is in the deal for a client or partner and then get talking to people.

Money costs – LIBOR sets the rate

The banks can 'buy' money for a fee. The average interest rate calculated on a daily basis is called the LIBOR rate (London Interbank Offered Rate). This is best explained as the interest rate that banks pay for the money they borrow. They can choose to borrow money for set periods and LIBOR has rates for three or six months, and one or more years. It is quite interesting to look at these rates and see how they change over time. Analysts use this information as a measure of the confidence in the market and to predict future interest rates.

So, if you want to borrow from Birmingham Midshires, their primary bank HBOS may have actually bought or borrowed the money they are lending to you on the open market. Let's say they are being charged 2.5% – they need to make a profit on that money. They have to cover their business costs.

Let's say that to lend you £100,000 it costs the bank 2.5%, *plus* they have to pay staff, systems, premises and marketing. Assume they need to charge about 9% to cover all these costs and make a profit. Now they can't charge 9% when the base rate at the bank of England is just 0.5%!

So, they charge a fee of 3% to cover 'administration costs':

£100,000 x 3% = £3,000

If you divide that evenly over 12 monthly mortgage payments, that is like paying another £250 a month – it's a good job you can add it to the loan!

So, if your real mortgage rate is 4.49% and you take out the borrowing on a one-year term, then in effect you are paying a rate of closer to 7.45% (as you add the 3% fee to the mortgage rate). If the tie-in period for the mortgage is two years, then you can apportion the admin fee over the two years so, in real terms, your mortgage rate would be 4.49 + 1.5 = 5.99%.

The bottom line is banks that have lost lots of money in the past, need to make a profit now. Some have a massive business debt to repay the taxpayer! This is why there is this tension between the Bank of England's low base rate and relatively high lending rates, coupled with (in my opinion) high lender fees.

When you take out a loan, consider the cost of the lender fees alongside your interest rate and the term of the tie-in period of the loan. Initially, you will probably want a one-year mortgage rate to enable you to remortgage the property and circulate your cash investment. When you are ready to remortgage, you will need to consider your strategy and attitude towards risks, as well as the overall performance of your portfolio before you can decide which new lending product is most appropriate for your needs.

I would suggest that you choose the longest term you can get, with the best rates of course, that meets your strategic needs. The long-term products will help you to spread the cost of the high lender fees over a longer period and effectively make the process of remortgaging cheaper. However, this does not necessarily mean that you have to have a fixed rate – that is a choice based on interest rates.

As a final point, LIBOR and banks buying money on the open market explains why you are charged early redemption penalties. The bank will have borrowed the money it is lending to you from someone else for a set period. If you give the money back, then the bank is no longer receiving interest payments from you, yet will still have to pay them or re-lend the money with associated increased admin costs. The bank needs you to borrow the money for the same or similar period that they have borrowed it for. That is why certain lending products come and go in the market. The bank will have been able to borrow at a specific rate and when that money is all lent out, they will have to borrow again at a new rate – so creating a new lending product.

Why go commercial?

The best reason to go commercial is because the bank will consider you as a complete person or business, unlike mortgage lenders who see you as a credit score and a specific property. They will also 'create' or offer you a lending product that is bespoke to the risk that you present. This means that the more successful they consider you and the lower risk you present, then the more preferential the terms of the loan.

Commercial lending or a buy-to-let mortgage – what's the difference?

The driving imperative for most investors to move to commercial lending is the change in tax allowance on mortgage interest – mortgage interest relief. Changed under Section 24 of the Financial Services Act – this graduated reduction in allowance has the larger investor transferring their portfolios to a limited company structure. As previously mentioned, this is such a personal matter I would not dare to comment directly here. The main thing to remember is don't panic and join a 'scheme', and don't pay a fortune for advice. Simply consider your investment plans and business model, consider your maximum personal income and then make an informed decision.

There is a difference in the philosophy or culture of the two types of organisations that's very noticeable.

When you start a conversation with a bank about commercial lending, they will want to follow a very similar process to a mortgage lender, but you will need to present yourself very differently. They will want to know that you are a safe business for the money they are going to lend you. They will check your credit score but, more importantly, they will meet you face to face and want to understand your business model, how it works, where you make money and why it is a good idea. You will need to explain and justify your strategy – this means you need your research and facts to hand.

Commercial lenders will want details of your existing business and investments, details of your income, expenditure, assets and liabilities. They will also want to know what cash you are going to put into the business or the deal. They are going to credit score you and also investigate your business model and your experience. As you can imagine, this is much more in depth and initially time consuming than applying for a decision in principle (DIP), but for some of you it might be worth being considered as a whole entity. If this all sounds too daunting, speak to your broker and explain that you want to approach a commercial bank. They will be able to help and advise you. If not, do it yourself. You have nothing to lose and everything to gain.

If you pass the 'interview' stage, the bank will want to know that they can obtain security for the money they are going to lend you. They will take, in principal, anything of a similar value. This means it does not have to be the actual house you are buying; it could be another unencumbered property or cash savings. In most cases, they will use the property you are buying and carry out a survey on it. They will demand indemnities and guarantees, so be prepared.

The terms for the lending are now negotiable! Which means, within reason, the better you are as a business proposition and the less risk you present, the more preferential the rates you can agree.

There are several components to a commercial loan:

1. The exposure or loan to value. In simple terms, how much is the bank prepared to lend you against the collateral you are offering? At the moment, they are mostly offering a maximum of 65%.
2. The cost of the money or the interest rate. Now, it is important to be careful here, because most commercial lending is on a capital and repayment basis, not interest only like with buy-to-let mortgages. They use phrases like 'pay rate'. A pay rate of, for example, 3.5%, means 3.5% over the base rate (which is currently 0.25%) giving a total loan rate of 3.75% capital and repayment (this will feel like a rate of more than 7% if it is an interest-only equivalent loan).
3. Coverage. This means that you must have sufficient income (rent) to cover the cost of repaying the debt. Banks express this as a percentage. In a normal buy-to-let mortgage, they look for 125% coverage, although lenders are increasing their multipliers. All commercial banks will be different but, essentially, they do not count the full annual rent as income, they assume a percentage of void and maintenance costs. So they may only consider 70% of rental income and then expect that to cover the loan cost by a rate of 160%, for example. You will need to really

understand this part of your agreement; otherwise, you may find that none of your deals will actually be acceptable.

4. Finally, there is the term of the loan. As with normal mortgages, this will be based on age. However, because the bank assumes that you will keep the loan and clear it in full through monthly payments (capital and repayment), then this can make your monthly payments quite high and in turn affect your ability to provide rental cover. They will refer to the amortization of the loan, how the capital portion of your mortgage reduces the actual debt.

Commercial lending is really easy to understand once you put yourself in the position of the lender. They want to lend money safely, knowing that you can afford to repay the debt and, if not, that they have sufficient security to recoup their money if necessary.

Why is commercial lending a good idea?

There are three great reasons:

1. Much cheaper fees. Unlike mortgage companies, banks do not charge 2–3.5% admin fees; fees can be just a few hundred pounds. However, the surveys can cost about £500 instead of £300.
2. Banks do not operate a 'six-month rule' on commercial lending. So they do not mind if the vendor only bought the property three months ago.
3. They do not charge 'early redemption charges'. Therefore, although there is a term (length) to the loan, you are not tied into that lending product like with buy-to-let mortgages.

Now consider points 2 and 3 together. This means that you could buy any property you like (providing it meets the lending criteria) and then either resell it on the open market or remortgage it after refurbishment at closer to its full market value at the six month stage, rather than waiting a year for the buy-to-let term to end.

Different is good

This is a different way of borrowing money and, like with credit cards, you need to understand what the lender wants to achieve and what they want from you.

1. Are you the owner of a sound business, well justified with appropriate experience?
2. Can you provide appropriate levels of collateral, either through other investment properties or assets of value?
3. Can you afford to pay back the loan? Can you prove that you can cover the cost of the debt through the rent on the property and through a partner's employed income?
4. Ultimately, the lender wants to know whether or not you are going to be a good customer from whom they can make money.

Certainly, in my case, they really liked the fact that Bob, my partner, was employed and had a regular income – this provided additional security and peace of mind. The bank obviously wanted us to transfer our business account to them – that was no problem. They were happy that we (temporarily) deposited a fair-sized cash lump sum in the account, which we later withdrew over a couple of months. The need to have a salary, reliable SA302s, and provable income within the business partnership is definitely becoming a requirement with most lenders.

Think like a professional investor, present yourself as a serious and knowledgeable business owner, show the bank you know what you are talking about and have a track record of success, or that you are planning to have a track record of success.

So what do lenders like HBOS and The Mortgage Works want?

The reason I started with commercial lending is because 'off-the-shelf' mortgage lenders like Birmingham Midshires (HBOS) and The Mortgage Works want the same things as commercial lenders. They want to know that you will pay them back and that they can make a profit.

The difference is that with HBOS or The Mortgage Works you are one of hundreds and hundreds of mortgage applications a day going through a massive centralised system. You are on a conveyor belt and they can pick and choose the best applications based on whether or not they have lent out all of the money that they planned to.

Rather than see you as an individual business with a business plan and strategy to back it, you are simply a way for them to hit their lending targets. Yes, you will get an interest-only mortgage, but this comes as a non-negotiable product (off the shelf) with tie-in periods and hefty admin costs. Depending on the size of your portfolio or future investment plans and your taxable income – normal off-the-shelf lending outside a limited company protective shell could result in you saving more cash than you might lose with the additional costs of limited company accounts. Both commercial and off-the-shelf lenders have a role to play – it all depends on your strategy.

Chapter 6

The rules – facts and figures

I will limit this chapter to just a series of headlines and pointers, as the detail is so volatile and changeable that you will need to check *everything* with your broker.

As it stands at the moment there are a series of rules, conditions and considerations that you need to take into account when costing the finance for any specific deal. To some of you, this chapter will not be news. But for many of you, this will be very valuable and possibly save you from a dreadful deal.

I was recently talking to some investors who I considered quite experienced. In the process of the conversation, they explained a specific deal, which was a redevelopment they planned to sell on within two months of purchase – this was when I realised that there are still investors not aware of all of the ins and outs of financing a deal.

The six-month rule

During 2008, lenders started to clamp down on the process of buying a property at discount and then immediately remortgaging it at market value. The famous and classic system was with Mortgage Express. It was initially used on new-build developments, but soon started to spread to existing houses as the market moved away from off-plan and new build.

All no money down (NMD) strategies are designed to get around the fact that lenders only want to lend you a percentage of the purchase price.

The actual rule was recommended by the Council of Mortgage Lenders and adopted over time by lenders. The rule means that a lender will not lend money for the purchase of a property where the vendor has not already owned it for six months.

The crucial date for most lenders is the date of completion and this is required to be recorded on the Land Registry. Now this is an optionally adopted rule and most commercial lenders are not bothered by this, whereas nearly all high-street, off-the-shelf lenders do apply the rule. You must be aware that this rule applies to investor *or* residential buyers, especially using the HBOS group and the other buy-to-let lenders.

Early redemption charges or penalties (ERC/ERP)

Most off-the-shelf lenders will want to know that they have lent you money for a specific time. This is nothing to do with the term of the mortgage, usually between 15 and 25 years. This is to do with the commitments they have made to borrow that money from the money markets.

An ERC or ERP varies from lender to lender and, for example, might be 3% of the loan if the loan is redeemed in the first year of the product term, reducing to 1% in the third year of a product term.

You must check the tie-in periods of any mortgage product that you are considering; otherwise the projected profit or cash released on remortgage can be significantly less.

Again, there are a number of lenders who do not charge ERC, these are mostly building societies. With the benefit of no ERC comes the 'penalty' of a higher interest rate or a lower loan to value. This is something to consider carefully in your calculations.

Putting ERC with the six-month rule

So, if your intention is to buy, refurbish and sell a property in under a year, the following conditions would need to apply:

1. To locate a mortgage product without a tie-in period and therefore no ERC.
2. To understand that any remortgage or sale of the property would need to be funded by a lender who did not operate under the six-month rule.
3. Or wait six months before you complete on the sale.

This means that the majority of people who are looking to buy and get 'all their money back out in six months' have not really considered all the constraints on that strategy. The hardest hit are builder-developers, who turn a derelict property back into decent home standards!

Remortgaging takes 12 months not six

Remortgaging will be affected by the six-month rule in the same way. The first purchase loan must be a product without ERC. Then the second 'remortgage' lender will need to offer a mortgage product that does not require you to have owned the property for six months or more.

If you are looking to release significant equity to get your investment cash back out into circulation, you will also need to consider the surveyor companies that lenders use. Each surveyor will have a patch and they will know the properties and their histories. Without significant upward movement in the market, you will be unlikely to release £30,000 for just a coat of paint. The surveyors have long memories and will want to see capital improvements.

The cost of bridging

I have yet to find a deal, personally, where the profit is still significant enough to take the risk of buying using bridging finance. Remember that the combination of the six-month rule and lender awkwardness means that you must budget and plan for at least nine months (in my opinion), otherwise the penalties could be crippling.

Work carefully with your broker to make sure that all of the numbers stack up and that your profit projections have included sufficient contingencies, then double-check these figures with the brokerage house. Make sure that you have worked through and understood all of the costs.

Cash out – I base my figures on 2 for 1

I mentioned in the Introduction that someone contacted me and asked for a copy of all my deals over the last year, as they had not been able to find a deal where they could get all of their money back out in six months. Even without the additional constraints applied by mortgage lenders, this strategy requires a stable or rising market to guarantee success. I am not sure exactly what is happening as you are reading this book, or the tangible and implied impact of Brexit, but I bet that the market is still vulnerable and volatile! The cash out strategy not only relies on prices holding, but also requires a surveyor to agree with your calculations one year in the future. I can't rely on a surveyor to confirm a price on a month-by-month basis.

When I demonstrate my projections to clients, not only am I extremely cautious, but I also estimate *no* increase in property value (as caused by normal inflation, which is running at approximately 5%), no change in loan to values calculations and just the average street value less £5,000 (contingency).

I would rather a client, or myself, came to remortgage a property and was delighted that they had managed to pull most of their money back out, rather than risk disappointment.

I have a demonstration that shows clients the potential income and ROI from an investment pot of £200,000. It assumes that the money pulled out at the one-year remortgage is only half of the total buying costs. Remember, I assume buying costs to include solicitor fees, surveys, my fees, right through to refurbishment budgets, gas certificates and tenant find fees. I feel this is a more realistic set of figures to use. If the deal works on this basis, then it's a good deal.

Below market valuations (BMV) and surveyors

This has really been covered earlier, but I can't miss an opportunity for a moan about this strategy and the surveyors. I mentioned that surveyors can't be relied upon to agree with your figures. In fact, if you challenge a surveyor and they give in and agree with your valuation, then that impacts on their insurance.

Valuations are so subjective, yet really they shouldn't be. I have just had two surveys by the same lender and same valuation company on the same property. The result… one surveyor wanted a retention to repair the chimney leading and the gutter (£2,500 for just £250 of work!), the other never mentioned the roof and wanted an electrical report!?

At one point, I had four purchase surveys and two remortgages taking place all on the same day with the same lender. The properties were in four different areas of the city; they included three houses and three flats. There were three surveyors and the one carrying out the remortgages was greeted at the property and offered a pack of local comparables. Every single property (all six, in four different areas, with three different surveyors and two property types) came back exactly £5,000 less than the requested valuation figure. How is that possible?

Ultimately, like the banks, surveyors got carried away with themselves and the rising property market in the mid 2004–2007. They overvalued the assets and under-considered the rental implications of large blocks of city-centre flats. This is effectively a double backlash; first against past overvaluations and second against the actual availability of funds. You just have to live with it. No doubt you saw details of the court case in 2011, where the court ruled that 'a surveyor was employed by the lender to carry out the valuations on their behalf and *did not* owe the purchaser a duty of care'. Okay, so that is surveyors well and truly dismissed and disgraced!

To finish the topic of valuations and surveys, have you come across the deal packagers that offer you a property at 30% BMV and all your money back out in…? Or worse, they packaged the financials too and made the deal NMD? I won't labour my opinion about the legalities, other than to say there was a significant increase in the number of reported fraudulent attempts to gain mortgages and discovered fraudulent mortgage applications from mid 2011 onwards. Worse than fraud, this strategy reduced the so-called investors' cashflow and created a portfolio of highly-geared properties.

Lease options – the rules still apply

This is still a relatively new and untested strategy in the UK. The early structures sent investors down a lease pathway that meant they could not complete on the deal in three, five or seven years time, because of the six-month rule and the deal structure needed to resell to a tenant buyer on an assignable contract. If you don't understand what I have just said and you are currently pursuing a lease option strategy, you might need to get advice and check how you are structuring your deals.

I have also mentioned lease options, where I commented that this strategy (and you could argue any strategy) takes a lot of time to get right. I think a lease option strategy takes longer to get right because you are effectively speaking to desperate and distressed people at a time of high emotion about a new form of finance that is not widely understood in the UK.

I would really urge you to consider all the same buying rules for a property as you would if you were going to proceed with a purchase and a mortgage. By taking on these leases, you are taking on the commitment of the property. You need to be clear that the monthly return will give you significant income in return for your time.

I know some lease option trainers talk about 'tenant buyers' taking on all the responsibility, but as with the words 'passive income', there is no such thing as something for nothing. This tenant buyer still needs monitoring; after all they are actually your asset – not the property because you don't own that! The money is in the hands of the tenant buyer!

So why do you need buying rules for lease options? Because at the end of the lease term you still need to make this deal work as either a purchase or sale. If you are going to buy it yourself, will the property cashflow as a rental under the new increased mortgage? The mortgage will increase because the rates will change. If you are planning to sell, who is your target vendor and can they afford to finance the purchase? Not every deal has a tenant buyer in the mix. In the meantime, you still need to cover the cost of the current owner's mortgage, insurance and possibly repair costs and void periods while making a profit. How much do you need or want in exchange for your time and possibly your stress?

Remember the basics…

These are just some of the headline facts and figures, rules and conditions you need to consider on any deal that you are thinking of buying. Run the numbers – overestimate costs and underestimate profits – if the deal still works, great, it sounds a beautiful one. If the numbers are borderline, recheck and reconsider. I remember a quote from Sir Richard Branson, 'Businesses are like buses – there is always another one coming along…'. I think properties are like buses; there is always another one coming along. It is better to miss one and get a comfortable seat than to spend the next 2–3 years chasing it down the street as it leaves with all your money.

Summary

I was very conscious when I came to the end of this section that it was much briefer than Section 1. Does this make it less important? Definitely not! It means that the economic environment is much more volatile and that is the one big disadvantage of writing a book – the time delay in publishing. Once written, life moves on and the words remain static.

I hope you recognise as you read this section that you will have to double-check everything for current relevance. My aim in mentioning all of the issues that are current now (some that may have already passed their time and some that may be still to come) is that you will have a broad base of understanding from which to conduct your own research.

So now we are at a point where you understand 'why' you want to invest. You have a critical understanding about money – how it flows, how it can be leveraged and how it can be measured to ensure return on that investment is the best possible use of your valuable resource. You also have the language of the lenders, whether they are banks or private individuals, and can demonstrate and explain why your investment opportunity is one not to be missed.

Now it's time to move on to the practical section – Section 3. Whether you are brand new to investing or have been buying for some time, Section 3 will take you through the process that I use to source properties step by step. Remember, I am my number one client, then my family's, joint venture partner's and my bespoke clients'. That does not mean that my bespoke clients get second-best deals or that I keep all the best deals for myself. Whoever has the money to invest is the person I shop for.

I buy properties to order. I do not randomly get deals and then try to place them. This means each person, myself included, gets the best possible deal available at that time. My time is very focused and each minute spent sourcing is paid for by a client or myself. I use my time wisely and find deals that use the investment cash wisely.

SECTION 3

Becoming a property
business owner

Chapter 7

Getting practical

This section of the book contains the essence of how to set up and run a property business, by thinking and acting as the owner of a property sourcing business. Depending on your skills you could apply this concept to running a rent-to-rent business, assisted sales or development business. The model and purpose of this book is designed to:

- streamline your time, making it more effective and financially rewarding

- sharpen your focus on the best possible cashflowing deals

- leverage all available resources – yours and other people's.

It is a simple model… based, of course, on a sound understanding of all the principles that have been described in the first two sections.

Just in case you have skipped forward to this section, I highly recommend that you take onboard the business concepts in Section 1 and the financial language and understanding of Section 2. Otherwise, I believe that your path to financial freedom will have a lot more bumps than necessary!

This section is now going to move through all the stages of finding and selling a property deal.

Getting started:

- Set a budget.

- Choose the right strategy, yield and cashflow.

- Understand how the figures work.

- Find the right area.

Defining the area to property type and tenant type:

- Visit the area.

- View a house or two.

- Understand estate agents.

- Draft your list of property buying rules.

- Understand letting agents.

Running the numbers:

- Work out the true value of a property.

- Tips from a surveyor.

- Make an offer.

- ROI examples.

Building relationships:

- Understand your personality type.

Understanding the service you are offering:

- Decide what service to offer.

- Decide what to charge.

- Find investor clients.

- Establish the relationship.

The contract and paperwork:

- How you get paid – what you get paid for.

- Securing the deal.

- What to do if it all goes wrong.

- What not to do.

Doing it all again, moving to the next level:

- Outsourcing.
- A brief word about systems.
- Reputation and marketing.

Ready?

Setting the marketing budget and creating a business plan

Before you even start your business of investing it is going to cost you money, so you need to create a business plan – an income and expenses chart. Put in the amount you want to earn monthly (net) and then a budget for expenses. It does not matter how much you need to earn a month net, the figure is a tool to calculate how many deals you need to source and sell on. So if you wanted to earn £2,500 net per month and had expenses of £500 per month, then you need to source at least one property per month at £3,000.

I would suggest that you set a minimum marketing and research budget of £2,500–£5,000 per annum and plenty of time. You need to be sure that you can 'afford' to start this business financially and in terms of your commitments. Knowing these numbers helps to give you focus on what you need to earn; your business plan will help you to be focused on budgets, income and expenses. It did take me a while to understand how it was possible to create a business plan when I did not know the sales price of a property, but that's because I was focusing on the wrong thing. Your business plan simply states how much income you must generate to cover expenses and still leave you with a net profit – so, in effect, how many deals you need to source or properties giving you cashflow you need to own.

In your marketing/research budget you will need to allow money for travel and accommodation, depending on where your areas for research turn out to be. You will need money to buy food while you are there if you are staying over.

How much time can you spare? Are you working full time? When will you fit in your research? Are you prepared to use your annual leave to visit your chosen area for research and then later to buy deals? How much time can you take off work? I think the biggest thing that people miscalculate is the cost of personal time. Not just in this initial phase while you are all excited, but ongoing over the next two years while you build your connections, not only with contacts in your chosen area but also with those who will invest – your future clients.

If you can't commit for the first year to the following, then maybe you need to consider how seriously you want this new business:

- At least one evening a week networking. Pick one or two regular events that you can go to each month and then travel to other events to meet new people and see different areas. Budget for this is £960 over the first six months (four meetings at an average cost of £20 – which you may be able to reduce by pre-booking), plus a small budget for pre-meeting and post-meeting socialising in the bar (this is vital as it is where a lot of business happens, but you can drink a soft drink!) and travel costs.

- Saturdays – to research your area, track property prices, spot new properties for sale and analyse deals.

- Then, I would say, once every three weeks minimum take a trip to your area for a day. Ideally, do this during the week, but not Mondays as many estate agents have sales meetings first thing. Find the days your agents offer viewings and visit then. This trip can easily scale back to once a month, once you have a relationship with the estate agents but it should be supported with calls and emails between visits.

- Each visit would have a budget of £50 per night for accommodation (maybe less depending on where you are in the country), £50–£100 round trip petrol or transport costs, then a budget to eat while away from home, as two-day-old homemade sandwiches are nasty. Say, two nights – giving two full days on location for the first six months. Fifteen visits at about £250 each is £3,750.

Okay, let's move on to the area – you can always refine the budget later once you have chosen your target area and worked out the costs more precisely.

More assumptions

The whole of this third section will assume that you are starting a sourcing business and then going to use your success to build it to a point where in 2–3 years (once you have appropriate accounts – and that is really important) you can give up work – safe in the knowledge that you will still be able to acquire mortgages.

If you have a secure relationship with a life or business partner, you may be able to move this date forward and rely on them as the core mortgage host for your own personal portfolio. By mid 2011 lenders were already requiring property investors to cover rental income with a supplementary PAYE salary in excess of £20,000–£25,000. 7 July, 2016 saw the European Parliament bring in new regulations regarding the evidence require to prove mortgage affordability on buy-to-let mortgages.

As lenders may not consider rental income as part of your accounts, you will need to source deals or have some other business-related income – that is why sourcing is a brilliant combination of focus and financial evidence. To earn £30,000 profit, you will need to source approximately 15–20 deals at £5,000 each subject to expenses and costs. This profit either covers your home costs (through wages) or is providing the start of your personal investment pot (pure profit). I also assume that you are planning to develop and refine your sourcing business and then take it to the next level. It is vital that you do not make decisions about 'early retirement' without securing your future mortgage-ability first and that will take accounts with profit!

Choosing the right strategy – I know why, now how do I start?

So how do you get started? I will assume that you are going to start with a relatively easy 'cashflow' model of investing – finding properties with a great ROI for investors looking to benefit from better cashflow for their money.

The reason I am starting with this strategy is that cashflow is everything. We are at a time of unprecedented low interest rates so this is the best time to benefit from high cashflow and, if you can't get it from a deal now, then is it really a great deal? Also, with a slow sales market and flatlining house prices, any refurbishment and quick flipping strategies for capital gain is a challenge, even before the lenders apply their rules and conditions.

Then there is the tax advantage – to buy, wait for appreciation and remortgage is effectively tax-free money to shop again. To buy and sell, is a taxable gain, which means that when you reinvest your cash in the second property it is 20–40% less than the profit you made on the first house! And I have to end with my opinion that buying to sell is a high-risk strategy – I want 'guaranteed' returns.

Yield and cashflow

If we are looking for high cashflow, then the first financial tool that I would use to define where in England I would buy is yield. Yield takes the gross rent per annum and divides it by the sale price on a property-by-property basis (you can average this for an area). Personally, I would look for areas where the yield is at least 10%. What you will be able to see if you are moderately good at maths is a pattern emerging. Rent needs to be high in proportion to a low-ish purchase price. Let me show you some examples:

Monthly rent	Annual gross rent	House price	Yield
500.00	6,000.00	100,000.00	0.06
500.00	6,000.00	75,000.00	0.08
550.00	6,600.00	65,000.00	0.10
600.00	7,200.00	100,000.00	0.07
600.00	7,200.00	75,000.00	0.10
700.00	8,400.00	75,000.00	0.11
700.00	8,400.00	200,000.00	0.04

You can already start to see a pattern. Where can you find rents on a buy-to-let property that are between £550 and £700 (or more) per month, but equally house prices that are low at £65,000 to £75,000? (Remember that this is the 'asking price' if you are working this out using Rightmove or Zoopla.) You can start to refine areas and assume a moderate discount on purchase price afterwards. Starting this way finds an area and buying a property under the asking price means that you will be able to find an even better corner of your area.

How do the figures work?

I spoke about yield as being the first 'financial tool' you can use to find an area, but by simply using Rightmove you can locate areas that meet your buying requirements. In fact, I no longer use yield as a measure after making that first decision. I personally find that yield lacks the level of true cost detail that I want when making a decision to buy a specific property.

For example, two properties both costing £60,000 and both giving a rental figure of £500 per calendar month would give the same yield:

£500 x 12 = £6,000 (annual rent)

£60,000 (purchase price)

= 10% yield

What yield does not factor in is the cost of refurbishment, if required, to achieve the market rent of £500. One property might have double glazing, gas central heating, a good kitchen and bathroom. It might only need a little decoration and some carpet costing, say, £1,500.

The other property might need double glazing, a new kitchen and full redecoration costing, say, £7,000. That would bring comparative costs to £61,500 verses £67,000. That's why I use ROI as my ultimate financial weapon. This figure explains, on a buy and hold strategy, exactly how much the money you have invested has earned you in rental payments (the equivalent of interest if the money stayed in the bank). It will also factor in any differences caused by loan to values and interest rates, because it considers the actual money earned and compares that to the actual total money spent.

The formula for ROI is:

Net annual rent = rent – (mortgage, letting agent fee and insurance cost)

Total cash invested = deposit + (solicitor's fees, survey, broker fee, refurbishment costs and tenanting costs)

Using this formula, I can compare a wider range of properties in one broad geographic area until I find the specific property types, number of rooms, level of refurbishment, even the streets I want to invest in.

What lies behind this formula is an understanding of the cost of money, and how leveraging money enables an investor to borrow from a wider range of sources while benefiting from the ongoing monthly cashflow. This is so important that I will come back to the numbers again in detail later, as the more times you read this the easier it will be to understand.

Start with the internet and find the right area

Start with Rightmove or Zoopla as two of the better sites – you can either be systematic and write geographic locations down on a list and work through them, or you can start with places where you have been (that's how I started) or places nearest to you and then work outwards.

Enter the location address in the search box, this can just be the name of a town or area and select 'houses' and 'three bedrooms' as your filters to start – mainly because there is not a lot of difference in some places between two and three bedrooms when you compare it to rental income, size of property and potential future developments and strategy options. Literally do the same (I find it easier to use a second window) with rental properties (like for like).

Start looking for areas where a relatively low asking price is found in the same location as a reasonable rental value. Depending on how you start this strategy – the town you pick and where you live – you could find an area in two hours or two days. Think about it logically – think about how far you are prepared to travel.

I started by saying that you should find an area where the yield is 10%, just because you need to start somewhere. If you find an area relatively near to home that has a 8–9% yield, then that is great! As the slightly lower figure is off-set by time–cost savings and ease of working!

Once you have found a few areas (I would suggest maybe two or three) start to research the area itself. What is employment like? What are the council plans for area development, housing and businesses? There are loads of websites that you can use, including Mouseprice or Nethouseprices, local council sites, even local business sites and then, of course, the old-fashioned method of speaking to a human! Don't wait to find three areas before you get started – take action on this – put in the time. Don't fall into the 'analising' trap.

What type of property are you looking for?

This does depend on your strategy of course. For example, if you wanted to rent a HMO (house of multiple occupation) to students, then finding out the development and business plan of the university would be critical. The same principle applies to any investment, whether it is buy-to-let, commercial, a flat or a house. Who is your tenant type and what affects them? What can increase their 'value' as an asset? What could have a detrimental effect?

If you are going to target employed, maybe even professional, tenants, then you will need properties close to transport links or close to employment. You might also need parking if they are going to commute by car. Next, you would need to understand the industry and business they are in (for example, city workers, factory workers and hospital workers), so research the employer and other employers in the area. What are their plans? I would also consider the consequences of that employer closing down, moving or downsizing. What other work opportunities are there? Find out if local employers run a scheme to relocate their employees. Could you advertise on their notice board or intranet?

If your preferred tenant type is unemployed, then what is the council's system for housing people on the social housing list? How many are waiting to be housed? How does the council operate its benefit system? How does it set the local housing benefit rates? You will start to develop a picture of the local area, its employment opportunities and stability, the council and how it operates and the local housing benefit system (what it pays and how it works).

For example, in London you can (in some local council areas) become a landlord who supplies property to the council on a longer lease basis, for example, for 1–5 years. These schemes are very demanding, time limited and prone to cancellation at short notice so beware. The phrase used to describe this is 'Social Housing Landlord Schemes' or 'rent guaranteed schemes'. Once you have a relationship with the council, it can be easier to build up your reputation and the personal contacts necessary to provide a level of security for your properties and lease contracts.

This is the system that operates most of our London portfolio. Having said this, one property was cancelled with 24-hours notice and there was nothing I could do. If they don't need your property, they will just give it back!

In the north of England, a lot of councils have decided to work with local housing associations, contracting out the responsibility to house people on the social housing list. Many of these agencies will renovate or build and own their own stock, and so do not look to private landlords as a source of property.

In West London, there are a number of available schemes, from working with a specific local estate agent who manages the process, to some in-house council schemes that provide incentives to take higher risk tenants. Think about your strategy – your clients – the management of any problems – how quickly can you fill a vacant property? What ongoing skills and time commitment will your client need to manage this type of property?

Narrowing down the areas

As you work through your area research, you will naturally develop your strategy and refine your area. Don't get distracted and keep coming back to why you are doing this – cashflow! I got repeatedly distracted as I learnt about new strategies – HMOs, lease options, etc. Remember what you are looking for. All these other strategies are tools that you can apply *if* your main strategy does not work on a particular property. I very rarely bother and once you find what works, just do it again and again. Why waste time?

Depending on how much time you put into your research strategy, you could be ready to visit an area within a week. Once you see a place in real life it may send you right back to your desk research. The great thing now is that you can visit an area virtually through Google Street View, so take a virtual tour first to avoid any shocks or wasted trips.

Google Street View, again, is a small step in narrowing down your wider choice of areas – remember to take a look down side roads and around the back of properties if you can. Check out the employment areas, the shops, the schools and the various residential areas. You will be surprised where the camera cars have been. Remember, broadly speaking, each 'town' will have an area preferred by students, the affluent, families, professionals and unemployed – see if you can mark these out on a map.

Recognise that, depending on where you currently live, some parts of London and England are very deprived, run down and have high levels of unemployment. I believe that we can regenerate an area one house at a time providing decent housing for families and children and decent investments for astute investors. Councils certainly don't have the budgets! Having said this, you don't need to start investing right in the middle of a war zone. Choose the edge of a planned regeneration area, understand the council's plans and realise the effects of the austerity measures on these plans and their timescales.

Now for the real visit

If you still like the sound (and sight) of an area, then it is time for a visit. This visit will have two purposes: one to check local research and 'get a feel for the place'; and two to make contacts. I would suggest booking into a local, cheap hotel and staying over at least one night as you want to be able to have a drive around after dark. You want to check out morning traffic flows and see your area in all its glory at different times of the day.

By staying over you will also have more flexibility in making appointments to see people. I would suggest that most estate agents or letting agents will be happy to see you when you walk through the door. However, you may need to book an appointment to speak to the local councils.

Plan this visit carefully – think about what you want to find out, confirm or rule out. All the time, keep your tenant type in mind. Much of this is personal choice or, dare I say, prejudice. I initially set out to house professional tenants, so I wanted property on easy transport links to local areas of employment or relatively near local employers.

I assumed that people travelled to work by train, like in London. In fact, local buses were the transport of choice and this widened the search area for investment opportunities. I then started to speak to local agents and viewed properties in keeping with this strategy – the numbers did not stack up. Vendors wanted too much money; they knew the perceived value of their assets in terms of yield and were not necessarily desperate to sell at a discount.

As my area knowledge increased, I discovered that the local housing system operated on a points system, which meant that the average unemployed person had to wait ages for a property. They still had growing families and needed homes. The local housing allowance (LHA) actually paid more, in certain areas, than the private rental rates, because the benefits office used an 'averaging system' to calculate the rates. So once I found a property in an area where LHA rates were higher than local rents, I had a potential benefit tenant catchment area.

I will add a word of caution here: I only decided to pursue this strategy because I developed a relationship with a local expert who knew the system and the local tenants extremely well. This is a more risky tenant type, but can also be a very profitable one. Housing benefit tenants is a time-consuming, high-risk strategy for someone starting out – beware.

It is all part of the visit planning – why are you going? What do you need to know to decide if this area is the right area to invest in? This does not have to be hard academic fact – provable in a court of law – this is still early research.

When should you view a property?

This is a tricky question. I wanted to see the properties straight away – I was in a new area and in order for me to get a real 'feel' for it I wanted to see the inside of properties for sale and get a sense of what a local agent meant by 'in need of modernisation'. I love that phrase. Four words that can mean anything from 'needs redecorating' in West London to 'this property has no central heating, a new species of mould on the back wall and a tree growing out of the bedroom window' the further outside of London you get!

This, again, refers back to your budget – how much time and cash have you allocated to developing your business and researching your market?

Understanding estate agents

This is as important as understanding the lending market. I am assuming again that you don't have money to burn and that you are not an internet whizz-kid. Along with that, I am also assuming that you are not going to start placing newspaper adverts or developing lead generation websites from day one. Even if you do have these skills and/or lots of money, I would counsel against it until you are sure that your strategy will work in the area you have chosen.

So your first port of call is an estate agent. Their sole (and soul) purpose is to sell you a property. They want to work with professional people who know what they are talking about and keep their word. That should not sound daunting because you are professional – you are setting up your own property investment business. You do know what you are talking about and, more importantly, asking questions about because you have carried out your research and you have a specific reason for your visit – questions you want answering. You will, of course, keep your word – that goes without saying.

Now some estate agents (especially small local offices) will take time to talk to you about the area – offer you a cup of tea and see you as someone whom they want a relationship with. Others are hardnosed commission-making money machines. If they don't recognise you as having cash in your pocket (burning a hole right now), then you will get a degree of 'don't waste my time' attitude.

Remember, they are employees; in most cases, they neither own investment properties nor are looking to. They have been trained by the school system to be sales machines. They will be driven by targets and their commission. They will dress flash, have pointed shoes, trendy haircuts and, if they drive a car, it will be fashionable too! The estate agent chains will demand this through their company culture. The biggest difference is that you are taking control of your financial future and you will be financially free in the next 3–5 years.

They are employees and you are a business owner. You are there to interview them to see who you will pick to become your 'business partner', because as your business grows so will their commission! It's a variation on imagining them naked. I have interviewed my bank manager, my estate agents and my letting agents. I never told them obviously.

What does the estate agent need out of the conversation?

What does the estate agent want? The answer is easy – to know that you will help them to achieve their targets either for viewings or for sales.

What can you do to help?

See a few properties – maybe even make an offer or two. But *caution,* know that you can follow through if you get accepted. Personally, I would view half a dozen with each agent to find out the answers to the following questions (but I would not make any offers unless I had the cash to invest):

1. What are typical three-bedroom properties like in the area?
2. What are two-bedroom properties like?
3. What do the words in the description mean in reality?

4. What is the local construction like – is it Victorian terrace, or 1960s council?
5. Are gardens important?
6. Are most bathrooms upstairs or down?
7. What is the state of most kitchens and bathrooms in this price range?
8. What is the standard of décor?
9. Do local people prefer carpet or laminate, curtains or blinds, paint or paper?

Now, to get a balanced understanding of the local area you will need to view 'distressed' and possibly repossessed properties, mid-range family homes and maybe even something that is already under offer (find out the agreed price if you can). Be upfront, saying you are new to the area and want to find where your strategy will fit. Tell the estate agents what you are thinking of buying and who you want to rent to. Ask them the best areas.

I would repeat this process with at least four agents on your first visit. That's why you need to stay for two days maybe even two visits!

By the time you return home, you will have an amazing understanding of an area – how and whether it fits your strategy which agents you could maybe work with. I even received two email complaint letters when I placed under market value offers in an area where the estate agents felt they could sell for asking price – so what? I don't have to go to that estate agent again. I have to admit that at the time I was embarrassed, shocked and a thousand other feelings. BUT then I remembered that they were in a job and I was building a business and I need never see them again as they were just one of 10 agents in one area. So much of this business will be based on personality – you will love one agent and another person will loathe them – that's fine. Build *your* relationship based on *your* strategy for *your* business.

Time to review your research

I recommend that after your first visit you come back home and reflect on what you now know. You should have a starting area. You might change this in the future, but I would suggest that if it meets the following criteria, start the process of working out your investment model:

- Does the yield offer 9–10%?
- Do the cheaper properties sit in relatively decent areas where your tenant (not you) would feel at home?
- Have you found 2–4 agents who you could build a relationship with?
- Do you understand the local geography, employment and council area?

If you don't have enough information to decide on a local tenant type and appropriate property type, then you will either need to do more research or visit your second choice area.

When you do have enough information, you will need to refine the research further and create your buying rules. The rules make it easier for the estate agents and letting agents to understand exactly what you are looking for – it is, in a sense, your shopping list.

Your property buying rules

The rules bring everything together so far. At the beginning of this process, you needed to understand *why* you were planning to invest in property – what you wanted the result of property investment to be and your life to be like. Then you looked at the realities of your personal financial position. You have worked out the cashflow you want the business to produce, the level of involvement you want to have and your exit strategy. Now you need to draft out your list of 'property buying rules'.

My rules address the following issues:

- Purchase price – I personally want to buy below the £125,000 stamp duty threshold and so limited my stamp duty to 3% and I have defined this further as my area research helped me to create my investment model.

- Property type – I prefer houses as they often allow the opportunity for future development; you can't put a loft extension in a flat. Plus, I don't want to have a portfolio heavy with maintenance and service charges that I can't control, which is the downside of buying flats.

- Area – this is determined initially by yield and then strategy; it can be defined further by property type and tenant type and, of course, economic outlook.

- Number of rooms – I have calculated that a three-bedroom house gives a better return than a two-bedroom house (pound for pound), and a studio or one-bedroom flat attracts the wrong type of tenant in my area. Four-bedroom properties or above are okay for multi-letting, but this requires a high level of management that I do not want to be involved in on a long-term strategy.

- ROI or average net cashflow – this is crucial as it helps you to understand how many rooms are best suited to your strategy and whether it is buy and rent or multi-letting. Looking at the ROI figures lets you know how hard your money is working and whether or not this is a good use of that resource.

Once you have worked out your buying rules you can plan your second visit – this time knowing the property type, price and area you are looking for. You can test out your investment and see if you can find a property for your target tenant type, at the right price, that works for you or your client as an investment.

Take these buying rules (best kept in your head or notepad) and visit the estate agent contacts that you made on your last visit. Ask them for the sales details (the printed sheets) on properties they have available that fit your precise criteria (your property buying rules).

Don't arrange viewings yet. Go and visit the local letting agents and ask them for their opinion on your strategy. Show them the properties you have in your hand and, based on their comments, go back and arrange your viewings with the estate agents. Finally, go home and compare your new notes and numbers with all the information you have gathered to date, including the information from the earlier agent visits.

Letting agents

One other thing I would recommend you do while you are in the letting agent is obviously find out about their service and charges and effectively interview them as a potential business partner. Find out how they handle repairs and refurbishments. Do they use or recommend local builders? Do they have in-house staff?

Ask them questions such as how much will it cost to replace a bathroom, kitchen, decorate a property, fit a carpet or install central heating, etc? You can call a double-glazing company or two to get an idea on double-glazing costs. This will help you to build up a repairs and refurbishment schedule.

You will now have enough information to not only view the right property for your strategy in the right postcode, but you can start to calculate the ROI based on purchase price and refurbishment costs. You will also know the letting agent fees, cost of gas certificates, energy performance certificate (EPC) and tenant find fees. You have your investment model and can run the numbers to prove that it is a good deal for a client.

Chapter 8

Running the numbers – what makes a good deal?

You know what you expect to get from property investment and this is most likely cashflow (otherwise you would be reading another book!). You have carried out several days of desk research to narrow down your target investment areas. You have even been on location, 'got a feel for a place', met key future team members and now settled on *one* place. This is just the start…

I don't know where you will choose, but I do know that it will have hundreds of postcode areas (well, maybe not hundreds but certainly a lot). I have already suggested that you map out where different groups of people live (this sounds awful – sorry – but you need to understand the socio-geographic make-up of an area).

Next I am going to cover some of the actual maths to demonstrate, first, the difference between property prices and therefore areas and the impact on cashflow, and, second, the difference between property types and the impact on cashflow.

Before I do though, here is a brief recap on the impact numbers to consider:

1 ROTI – return on time invested

In Chapter 3 on page 51, I explained that understanding what your time is worth is critical in managing your time in a way that directs energy and effort towards balancing and increasing your cashflow. It can also help you to understand how much time a deal is worth. By this, I mean that if the deal is going to take lots of time to bring to the table, then I would want to be sure the returns are worth it. Remember my example of a coaching client who, prior to working with me, spent a year working on a deal to earn £200 per month.

So, if you have not already done so, calculate your hourly rate and as you work out the numbers and return on a deal think about whether you are going to be earning enough. Remember, the word 'enough' will be a different amount for each person and is based on your immediate and actual personal cashflow situation.

2 Yield

This is the first financial tool that you will use to narrow down your area, but it is very broad and does not help you to decide on a property type or specific location.

3 Below market valuation (BMV)

I have previously described this strategy as based on 'bulls*** values' because it requires a belief in fortune-telling, which is not a known business practice except at the funfair. What it does point to though is the importance of understanding what a valuation is and how to work it out. This is so *critical* as a skill that I will shortly discuss this point in some detail.

4 ROI

Understanding that the figures calculated by the ROI formulae are equivalent to interest earned on your money is vital in being able to evaluate deals and work out which deal is 'best value for money' or offers a better 'return' on your money – or that of a client.

Working out the true value of a property

We have all heard the words 'due diligence', but what do they really mean in the context of a property investment business? To me, the meaning comes in two parts.

First, the research that one puts in and continues to track about the area itself – what councils are planning, how government spending affects the plans for new roads or housing, the payment of benefits, the impact on social housing, prisoner release, vulnerable tenants or refugees.

Second, it comes down to the micro research carried out on a specific house that you are intending to buy or source for a client. That is what I want to focus on now because, if you guess an area but the numbers work on the property, you will make cashflow – for how long no one knows, but the deal will work. If you get the area right but buy the wrong property, you will definitely damage your cashflow potential and maybe even your long-term ability to hold the property. The key 'leveraging factor' about property investment is that you get the tenant to pay the mortgage. If there is no tenant or no rent, then you have to pay the mortgage or lose the property!

Alternatively, if you get the deal wrong and the rent does not cover the costs so there is no cashflow, then you are funding the mortgage. That is not leverage at all… in fact, that is not property investment. That is just buying lots of houses that you don't live in!

To value a property, many people will start with the sale price on the internet. This gives an indication of the *asking price*, which has no relationship whatsoever to the actual *sale price*. Actual sale price can be obtained through Land Registry or through certain sites like Nethouseprices, even Zoopla. However, it is already three months out of date at the point when you can access the information, simply because it takes Land Registry that long to update its data.

Value is determined by what you pay or are willing to pay for something and this is where I believe people get confused. Some prices are finite and non-negotiable, like your morning latte. Other items have negotiable prices like cars or art. There is a list or asking price and then, depending on your negotiation skills, there is a price that you will actually pay. You may even have that price in your head before you start the process, and that is a very good strategy to have. Other items, like foods nearing their best-before dates in a supermarket, are offered at a discount price because they need to be sold quickly or there is something wrong with the item – something has affected its perceived value.

So, if the internet displays the 'asking price' and that is not an indication of value or sale price, how do you work out the real value of a property? One easy way to do this is to 'employ' a local surveyor to talk you through their process – to teach you how they do it. I employed two local surveyors to survey a total of five properties (three properties each – one property was surveyed by both surveyors to check and compare their approaches and information).

I arranged that they would speak everything out loud to me rather than write a report. I learned about the local area in terms of geographical features (some areas have mines or Radon gas, others can be affected by subsidence or flooding), and the surveyors were an expert source. I learnt in one road that the flow of water during very heavy rain meant that all the basements on one side of the street flooded all winter. I learnt what cavity wall tie failure was and how it was treated. I learnt about damp-proof courses. The whole day cost me £500 and was worth every penny. Plus, I had five valuations and surveys.

I also learnt what surveyors consider as evidence of the value for a property and how they get comparisons. First, they look for sold prices, within three months, of like-for-like properties in the same road. If none exist, they might consider the road next to it, but local knowledge would tell you whether or not that was a true like-for-like comparison. One property I bought is worth £15,000 less than the road next door on a seemingly like-for-like comparison – similar structure and layout. Why? Because in the second road every house has a small open porch with a wrought-iron low fence and lattice work along the top of the porch. It makes the street look uniform and pretty and so more desirable; hence the difference in perceived and then actual value.

Top tips from surveyors

* Look at the internet to see the **asking price** for properties on sale in the road. If properties are being offered for less than your property, you will need to really understand why. Call the selling agent and ask about the property – even view it – it might be a better deal. It might have structural issues, be vandalised or be a repossession. (Repossessions are like 'creeping death' to the valuation of a street.)

- If one property is much **higher in valuation**, understand why. Most likely, the home owner has over extended and needs to clear the mortgage or has just got no idea! Know how long the property has been up for sale. On a road where I own a property, another carbon-copy house in a worse state of repair is on the market for £35,000 more than I paid for my property, and has been since the day I bought it! The owners want to move to a new-build flat in town and need £100,000 to buy it.

- Now visit Zoopla or similar sites like Nethouseprices and look for **sold properties**. Make sure you know whether the road has a mixed type of properties or just one property type. There is no point comparing a four-bedroom extended house to a two-bedroom original! Remember that properties in the same road (sold in the previous 3–4 months) would be considered a good comparison.

- If you have been working an area for some time, you will keep records of properties for sale in your area and know which agents sold them. You can then build or use your relationship with the estate agent to ascertain the actual sold prices much sooner than three months. As your **relationship with your estate agent** develops, you can ask them to check the Rightmove Professional site and tell you what has sold recently in the area you are looking at.

- **Know left from right.** There can be a big difference in house size, gardens and layout from one side of a street to another; ask your estate agent for some local knowledge.

- Finally, get on the phone. **Call local agents** and either:

  a) pretend you are looking to sell a property that great Auntie Flo has left you (be careful as I find this gets the sales people overexcited as they see a potential sale and so give you a higher valuation – you will have to explain 'quick sale' and 'offers in two weeks' to get them to lower their first valuation); or

  b) say you are looking for comps (comparisons or comparative prices) on XYZ properties, and hopefully they will tell you sold prices.

You will now have the following:

1. The asking price and an understanding of where your intended property sits in the range for that street and why.
2. The actual sold property prices that are three months old.
3. Possible sales, hot from the desk of your agent contacts.
4. An understanding of property types and differences on a street.
5. Comparables from local estate agents.

To calculate local values, I ignore the highest price and possibly the lowest if it appears as an anomaly – there are often reasons for these extremes. You will usually have a range, for example, between £45,000 (distressed repossession) and £150,000 (mad private seller) with a street value of around £90,000–£105,000. These example figures can be mirrored across the country.

Based on your knowledge gained through talking to estate agents, you will know whether the street is popular and a fast mover for sales (you will see higher priced property and they will be sold quickly) or a slower street. You will have driven up and down the road and the roads either side and opposite to give you a feel for it. You will have viewed the property itself and know its condition.

What you want to calculate, to the best of your ability, is what the property would sell for in a reasonable condition. On my streets, I would estimate a three-bedroom house with two reception rooms to sell for approximately £95,000 to £115,000, depending on postcode. I personally always take the lower value to be cautious, in this case £95,000. If you have a small defined area, then you will know your streets and your agents. You will already know the figure of £95,000 and then, in order to calculate your offer price, just deduct the cost of redecorating or a full refurbishment.

Offer price versus valuation

This is phase two. Okay, so in your head you know what the worse-case valuation is likely to be. You also know the asking price. Hopefully this is around your valuation figure, give or take 10–15%. Now what figure are you going to offer?

My offer price is already set. I know what price I want to pay – it is part of my buying rules. My rules 'tell me' the maximum price I want to pay for a two- or three-bedroom property because I want to achieve a certain cashflow and, therefore, can only afford to pay a certain price.

So, if my rules state that my top price for a three-bedroom property (including any refurbishment costs) is £95,000, for example, and the asking price is £105,000, then I would make an offer of £95,000 less the refurbishment costs of £7,500 – meaning an offer of £87,500. You might wonder why I have 'deducted' the refurbishment cost. If the house needs work, then in my opinion it is not worth the 'normal' price; having worked out the maximum amount I want to pay (£95,000), I then need to deduct any refurbishment costs. If the asking price was actually £115,000, then I would have to know more about the 'story' of the seller to understand how to negotiate. This is more of an art than a science – it's about information and relationships.

Making an offer

I am very honest with my estate agent contacts. When I arrive to view properties or call to arrange them, I let them know how many properties I want to buy and will casually mention if I am doing viewings with another agent. That way the estate agent knows the situation. Ultimately, it is all about making it easy for them to make a sale – not to waste their time.

Once I have viewed properties I will give the estate agents some immediate feedback, such as 'I like that' or 'OMG are you serious?' I will flag up 2–4 potential deals out of the 8–12 I have viewed that day (not necessarily all with one agent). I will let them know I am going to check some figures and then email or call them within 48 hours (depends where we are in the week).

That evening I will enter all my property data into my part-prepared spreadsheet. I already know the area value and rental income, so now I can add in the refurbishment costs and the asking price. From the spreadsheet, I can see what cashflow and ROI any given asking price would return.

If I hit my target cashflow, I would then be negotiating a purchase price just to get the best possible deal. If, when I enter the numbers, the cashflow is poor, then I know I need to offer a lower price. I use the spreadsheet to calculate this and I will reduce the offer price figure until I hit over £250 per month net cashflow, or an ROI over 10% – then I know how low I would have to go!

I will have already asked the estate agent the following questions:

- Who is the vendor? Is it a private sale (which can be expensive) or a probate sale (they can be greedy)? What about the landlord (often they can be over stretched)? Or is it a repossession (which is fixed price and very structured)?
- When did the property come to the market? (If it's early days, then the vendor is unlikely to accept an offer. You can still make one, but just don't be surprise if the answer is 'No'.)
- How many viewings have there been? (If there have been lots and no offers, there is often a story here – there is either something wrong with the house or the vendor!)
- How many offers have there been? (As above, there can be a story here.)
- I then always ask (maybe because I have a good relationship with the agents) what is the lowest offer that the vendor is prepared to accept? This gives me a guide – I don't always stick to it though.

Sometimes I let the estate agent know my workings out and why a deal just won't work for me. They can give feedback to a vendor and sometimes the asking price is reduced. Often the property stays on the market at the asking price for ages until the vendor reaches that desperate trigger and accepts an offer.

Typically, the offers I would make would be around my maximum purchase price rule or lower. I don't bother to calculate my offer based on a percentage of asking price, as I found that it gave me a false figure to work on. This was because if I estimated the street value incorrectly and then offered 25% below it, I might still be above my buying rule. I offer a price in order to get the cashflow; after all, I want this to be a long-lasting, successful business!

Rules and gut instinct

I do operate a lot of my business now based on instinct; it's a bit like riding a bike and feeling your balance. When I first started, it was very much by these rules:

1. Know my street values.
2. Know my buying rules – maximum purchase price I am willing to pay to get my target cashflow.
3. Build my relationship with my estate agent and know how to speak to them.

Start by using your rules and stick to them. As you get a feel for them and the area you are working in, you can start to bend, expand and reshape the rules and test out where the breaking point is. Find out where the deal breaker is and then operate below that line. When I say 'test out', do so simply by expanding the range of properties you view not by actually buying them!

ROI examples

Understanding ROI is crucial to making your offers at the right price. You need to know that the cash you (or your sourcing client) intend to invest will provide a good return. ROI is the only mechanism that can tell you this.

First, consider flats, they have an additional service charge for the overall maintenance of communal areas of the property – you will still need to maintain the inside of your own property. Depending on the state of the management accounts and the quality of the property, this can be a costly expense that you have no control over.

In 2015, one of my original London flats fell due for a seven-year major works repair schedule – it cost the block over £8m and my share was £8,500. Thank goodness interest rates had fallen, as this was over £630 per month from my net rent. I had no say or control over this work – it was carried out in accordance with the lease by the freeholder! Luckily the property still cashflowed at the end of it. If this cost had been apparent at the point of purchase the ROI would have been too low to warrant the investment.

The second example of hidden costs is with HMOs. You need to be clear on the tenant type you are planning to attract as, whilst this may be obvious, a number of strangers will have to live under one roof with one or two bathrooms and one kitchen. Often when the tenant type is LHA, the only people who would live in shared accommodation are single males. In some deprived areas, as I have found, long-term single males can come with challenges like drug or alcohol abuse. Please don't write and accuse me of stereotyping – I do understand that everyone is different – I am just explaining what I discovered when I considered this option in my area.

HMOs in city centres or on transport links near universities or hospitals could attract working or student tenants, each coming with their own challenges. Students, by nature of their courses, work to a specific timetable. Complete on a property in December and it may not get a new batch of students until the following September – how are you going to budget for this? There can be higher refurbishment costs in between rental periods – have you budgeted for this?

Lastly, HMOs usually require the landlord to pay the bills – these costs are often included in the rent. The consequence for you is that those additional costs are coming out of your profit. Tenants do not see the bills and do not necessarily conserve energy as we might at home. Make sure you budget adequately for HMO utility bill costs; they certainly bring down the profit margin.

When you compare the actual cashflow of a buy-to-let at £300 and an HMO at £800 respectively, and then consider the costs, your ROI could be considerably less.

Now let's consider the area. When you look at the gross rent possible on a West London three-bedroom house, you are talking about £1,700 – over double the rent of a three-bed in the north. However, the purchase prices reflect this and when you consider the amount of money needed to 'buy' the investment compared to the rent, using ROI you can see that you get a better return further north.

In fact, you actually get better cashflow too. If you consider the £80,000–£100,000 you would need to spend (in deposit alone) to buy a property in London, you could buy two or three properties up north costing £30–40,000 each, and earn a combined net rent off all three properties of £900 – a better cashflow.

Using ROI as a measure to compare deals you can see why I moved my personal investment strategy from close to home to further north, where the purchase price and rental ratios work better. I did still set out on that first trip to look at student HMOs as I thought they offered better cashflow, but soon realised that I could get better cashflow (easier management) and 'any time' renting by focusing on traditional buy-to-let property and ASTs (assured shorthold tenancy agreements).

Look at the ROI on your deals and then start experimenting with property costs and potential rental income and see what you discover.

Narrowing down your search

Now that you understand ROI and how relatively simple the spreadsheet is, you can start to look at your area in more detail. Start looking at postcode areas. What is the difference in ROI between A1 B23 and Z1 Y23? What is the difference in social class, building type, access routes, schools, commercial and then rents and purchase prices?

You will start to narrow down a small group of postcodes, which in larger towns and cities will often be found on the outer circular road (there's always a ring road or boundary road of some sort). Look at Birmingham, Manchester, Rotherham, Stoke, Margate, Grimsby or Hull. You can even find sections of London that hold true. Once you have decided on 2–3 main postcode areas in your chosen town or city, go to another level of detail and start to find the specific streets that you favour.

Building relationships – the foundation to success

All the professionals I have mentioned: estate agents and letting agents, the build teams, insurance brokers, mortgage brokers and solicitors are a vital part of your team. Okay, that is obvious – maybe what we forget is what they want to achieve in the relationship and how they want to be treated.

I would still suggest that you effectively interview every one of them – you don't need to tell them that this is what you are doing though. Just engage them in conversation, knowing in advance that you are looking for key service deliverables.

I would create a job description for your ideal letting agent and estate agent, your ideal builder or broker and then as you speak to them score them against your criteria. Of course, you could just go on gut instinct. I still do that a great deal. The other 'choice' factor is a referral by someone you trust.

Build a relationship. Remember you are one of many people who they have to deal with. Remember to say thank you in words or small tokens. I take a bottle of wine and chocolates to my estate agent every time I complete on a deal. I invite them to dinner a couple of times a year.

Each member of my team is a business in their own right, but they are also a person who I actually like and so have conversations and remember important details about them.

What personality type are you?

You might be a really detailed person; you might be a 'people and feelings' orientated person. Think about your personality type. How do you like to receive information? Do you like pictures or do you prefer things to be written down? Do you text or call? Do you want the facts quickly or would you like to get to know me first?

Once you understand the person and personality type you are, you can start to be more aware of the people you speak to. Yes, if you understand how to create rapport, then do so, but be congruent. I certainly wouldn't even attempt a conversation about football or cars. My only connections to football or cars are an *Everything a Girl Needs to Know About Football* book (a gift) and I own a Renault Megane because I like the button that puts the roof down (which is only useful on the six days a year it is not too cold or wet!)

I have recognised that people glaze over when I start spouting numbers or go into too much detail. I also speak quickly and have conversations that go off on tangents, as I think of new thoughts. You might have noticed that trait in this book too! Now when speaking to new people I aim to breathe deeply, speak more slowly, be clear about what I want to achieve and be conscious of the signs they are giving off in terms of interest level or their own congruency.

As you move around the country, you will find people with different interests and priorities. Be sensitive to these among your potential team and among potential vendors. You might need to be brave as you first start out and ask questions. I believe that it is in our human nature to help, unless you catch a person at month-end when targets are not met and they are busy completing their commission statement!

I would counsel against walking into an estate agent and asking for a 30% discount on a property when you have no cash or clients. Build up to it. However, if it does all go horribly wrong, there is always another estate agent, letting agent, broker or even town.

Chapter 9

Understanding the service you are offering

At this point some of you will be bursting to go and buy the deals that you have discovered. If you have the cash to invest, great, off you go. However, I would still suggest that before you buy for yourself, you think through what you are specifically doing and how it can be of interest to other potential cash-rich clients.

If you want to buy cashflowing buy-to-let properties and either you are new to investing, have no personal cash to invest or have invested in the past but your money is tied up so you are looking for a new strategy – this is the chapter for you.

Think about the product you have: cashflow, cashflowing investment packages, a business opportunity for someone with cash sitting in a bank, building society or property. You can, for a fee, introduce them to (or sell them) the deal. This all sounds great, but in order to communicate the message of the opportunity you have, you need to be able to describe it in a way that would attract the people (clients) you are looking for. What problem are you solving for your client?

Think about who would want a cashflowing deal. If you are just going to sell the deal on its own, who would have the skills and contacts to successfully complete the purchase without your help? Personally, I am too much of a control freak to leave the completion, and therefore the success or failure of a deal, in someone else's hands! I recognised quite early on that if I only got paid on completion, then I had to make sure that completion occurred; otherwise I was working for nothing.

So I believe what I have is a 'service'. I help (project manage) people with cash to invest in cashflow property investments. When I think about who they are, what they do, what they know – I can then start to think about what interests them and therefore how to talk to them.

Who are your clients going to be? What sort of a 'sourcing' service do they need? What skills do they already possess and what do they need you to do for them? Now you can start to describe your 'ideal' client, you can start to describe the service they want (not what you want to offer – what *they* want!) You can also start to think about your cashflowing deals and how you can describe these to them in a way that meets their information needs and solves their problem.

I learnt that this tied in very closely with the point I made about knowing yourself. Do you talk about detail? Do you skim over detail? What does your client need? In my experience, I certainly gave too much information at the start – I almost overwhelmed my clients with facts, figures, details and images. I made it impossible for them to decide.

I knew that my clients did not have a lot of time or specific knowledge about the details of property investment, hence they needed my services. I originally thought that if I gave them all of the information I had gathered to decide that a deal was right for them as an investment, that I would save them time and give them reassurance. All I gave most clients was a headache and a near-impossible decision to make. Fortunately, most of my early clients were not into detail, so didn't read the stuff I sent them anyway!

I have now trimmed down all the detail of the information I share with clients to the bare minimum facts they need to know:

- Offer price.
- Monthly cashflow.
- Cash required to invest.
- ROI.
- A brief description of the house (mid terrace, three bedrooms, two reception rooms).

Once one of my clients decides, on that basis, that they either want to invest or have more information, then I can provide it immediately because I had it all along – I just need to give it to them in smaller chunks. On a first deal, most clients will want more information. However, as they start to recognise the benefit of the deals that you source for them, they will probably require less information.

I have a number of clients who have had minimal information from me, seen no photos and only visited the area after the first few purchases. They have bought four properties with me. I have had other clients who said they did not want the detail of the deals and then repeatedly became anxious just before and during the purchase phase, because actually they do not want the detail but they needed it! It's just that work commitments kept them so busy. I have one client who reads every word of the purchasing contract and one time even noticed that page 109 was missing when it was faxed over to them by the solicitor!

Work with your clients – have all the information ready and provide it as required by each client and their desire for detail, reassurance or time. Remember, it is your responsibility to present the best possible deal available at that moment in time. It is the client's responsibility to decide whether or not they want to invest and they need to carry out their own due diligence – they need to be responsible for spending their own money!

So what sort of service are you going to offer?

This may be decided by the contacts you have in an area; it may be decided by whether or not you are working full time. Ultimately, the question is how far through the purchasing and tenanting process will you be supporting your client?

You could:

• introduce the deal and then stand back.

• introduce the deal and support through to completion.

- support through to completion and project manage the refurbishment process.

- support completion, refurbishment and tenant find.

There is no right or wrong answer. I think it is a matter of:

- time – how much do you have?

- contacts – do you have any?

- passion – do you enjoy this?

If you don't already invest in an area and have not been involved in the refurbishment of properties before, then you could keep it simple to start with. You could just find the deals, supply a list of local agents that could manage a refurbishment, simply introduce your client to the 3–4 letting agents you recommend and then step out of the process at completion. It will certainly take less of your time, which means you can move on to your next deal more quickly. I would ask you though to consider the question of whether your clients can then take that property and make it cashflow, because without cashflow they won't see, feel and experience the real benefits of the investment opportunity.

If you already invest or plan to invest in an area, or if you are more confident about refurbishments, then maybe you would prefer to project manage more of the process. This will impact on how much you charge.

How much to charge

This is where you can fall back on your hourly rate and consider how long it will take you to find, negotiate, complete, refurbish and support through to tenancy, a complete property investment deal. Then the number of hours or days multiplied by your rate will give you an idea of a chargeable fee.

You may still want to offer a discounted rate to start with in order to attract clients and build your reputation. You may want to check out what others in the market or your area are offering. Remember, your rate is based on your service, your knowledge and expertise and, above all, your hourly rate based on your financial needs. So checking another person's rate is a benchmark, not an absolute piece of information.

It was only a matter of months before I realised that I had more deals than I could buy. However, I knew that I had the skills, contacts and track record to sell these on and so my sourcing business was born. I did, of course, 'faff' around for another three months before I actually offered a deal to anyone. I was stepping up my game. Initially I had the courage to buy for me and then my family, but now I was going to share my investment ideas with strangers. What if they knew more than me? What if they didn't like the deal? What if they asked a question I didn't know the answer to?

All of these fears are natural. However, they also constitute an expectation of a negative outcome that may not be realised:

1. If a client knows more than you, great. This is an opportunity to learn. They will be experienced, have properties already and you could work closely and grow your mutual businesses.
2. If they don't like the deal, that is fine – they don't have to buy it. Other investors will like the deal – think how to explain it and get to the point a lot quicker.
3. What if they ask a question you don't know the answer to? Then you would say that you will find out. People don't see honesty as a weakness, well nice people don't.

This business is all about relationships and communication skills and you can learn to get better at both, if you need to.

So how much should you charge? My answer is that it depends on what you do. As part of your research, speak to other sourcing agents in the market. See how they present their deals and how much they charge their clients, bearing in mind this will still only be a benchmark. There is a massive price range depending on the service that is provided:

- Lead generation – website generated – unqualified leads sell for £25–£50.

- Lead generated and part-qualified contacts can sell for £50–£200.

- Packaged deals – this has implied no money down (NMD) deals in the past, where clients pay £5,000–£7,000 and the dealer is often making a cut on the property price and sometimes property management. The client will have little equity or cashflow.

- Packaged deals – where the sourcing agent charges a fee (£5,000–£7,000) for sourcing and then retains a share in the property's future capital growth. (This feels like having your cake and eating it too, but some clients are happy to pay for this, which seems like a lot of money to me.)

- Source up to completion for £2,500–£7,000 – in London some people charge a percentage fee of 1–3%.

- Source up to tenancy. Again, either for a fee or a percentage as above.

Whatever you charge it has to work in the deal. There still has to be great cashflow for the client and, of course, the all important ROI. I charge £9,950 plus vat for a deal taken through completion, and refurbishment ready for tenanting. I have considered how much time it takes. I have considered my contacts and my track record. I have considered value for money and ROI.

My deals offer great cashflow and ROI for people who work and are dissatisfied with the current returns they are achieving. Some recognise the untapped resources they have at hand; some clients are retired or just buy outright for cash.

What about finding investor clients?

I know that there are so many people out there with money invested in the stock market, sitting in savings accounts, lying dormant in property, that really there is no reason not to find a client. I think it comes down to confidence, understanding your service and explaining the deal in a way that your prospective client wants to receive the information.

It also means developing a thick skin and not taking rejection personally! Remember that, although you have found a way to become financially secure, possibly even financially free in a few years time, some people, especially those trained at school and/or in jobs, need structure, need to work and may even fear change.

Some of your clients are working through an internal battle; they recognise that things need to change but maybe they fear getting it wrong, or simply listen to the news too much – that's okay – that's for them to resolve when they are ready. So, if they say no to a deal, it is not 'no' to you, it's, 'No I am *not ready* to make this change yet!' Your job is to share the opportunity with people – when they are ready they will come to you.

Network and grow your confidence.

I was invited by one of my networking groups to a business dinner and as I sat there at the table full of men, I found that I was in my element. I felt a growing confidence as I spoke about what I did – when asked as part of the round table introductions. One guest commented that he had £800,000 sitting in his account; another asked me what I would do if he gave me £1million. My little voice immediately wanted to crack a joke about buying an around-the-world ticket to go scuba diving. Luckily, I realised this question was half serious. I replied, 'It depends on whether you are looking for long-term investment returns or short-term gains. In the short term, I could probably offer 6–8% return' (never start too high), 'however in the longer term you could be looking at anywhere between 10–25% ROI, depending on your attitude towards the investments' (never mention risk).

The man nodded and made an 'mmm' sound. It had fallen silent on the table as everyone listened and then all of a sudden conversation picked up. A friend next to me lent over and whispered, 'He is just selling his multimillion pound business – he owns his own helicopter and a fleet of rare cars!' That's when I knew that people with money look just like us, just like my parents, my neighbour or the person in the shopping queue! Don't judge – speak. Just talk to people. In fact, even better – have a conversation and ask questions.

Ask questions with care

I remember one of my mentors saying that 'the person who asks the most questions, controls the conversation'. It is definitely a skill that can be learnt. 'Be interested not interesting!' There is a balance to be struck between drilling someone mercilessly for information and having a conversation that has an underlying fact-finding purpose. It can be as simple as setting an intention or goal for the conversation to remind you of what you would like to know.

'Do you have any money to invest?' is not the best way to start! 'How would you like to take this forward?' can be a good way to end.

People like to talk about themselves! Give other people a chance to talk about their hopes and dreams – what they like and what they want. Some will want to talk about what they don't like and what they don't want. It takes all sorts.

Establishing the relationship

If we don't speak to one another, we can't build a relationship with one another. How do you move from having a conversation to building an investment relationship? You ask the question.

It depends what is being said in the conversation, but there is always a point where you can ask the question, 'Is that something you want to move forward on? Or… explore? Or… discuss?' How about, 'What do you need to know now to make a decision?' You may not take the opportunity, because *you* are not ready, or you may pick up the vibe that the other person is not ready (which may or may not be accurate).

If you don't ask, you definitely don't get. It's as simple as that. If you don't ask someone if they want to talk to you about how you can use your skills and knowledge to help them achieve what they want in life, then you are denying them the opportunity you have – you are selfish!

After a series of shorter conversations (often networking at events or via email) a potential client will decide that they want to know how they can move forward. How long it takes the client to make this decision differs for everyone. We then usually have about a half hour conversation, which is really an opportunity for them to tell me what help they want. Depending on their circumstances, I will either help them to make money from their property knowledge through a mentorship or coaching, or meet them to start the process of 'shopping for houses'.

Getting to know the client

There will be lots of ways to do this. My preferred way – because it's my way – is to have a formal strategy session where we meet privately and work out what the client wants to achieve, in fact, everything that I have described in this book.

I take them through a five-step process, which culminates in a personalised investment action plan and the possibility of our working together. I understand where they are financially, what they want to achieve, and I know whether my model will work for them. For some, it does not and it's really important that one of you finds this out very early on! This is not a sales opportunity particularly – it is a personalised strategy development session that leaves my clients better informed and clearer about their objectives and opportunities.

I usually buy 'stinky houses', and I call them that because they often have damp – usually from a leaking gutter – or they smell dirty or empty. They will mostly have been repossessed and left in a poor condition. I buy houses because I still want the opportunity to circulate my money, and that of clients, through an optional remortgage after 12 months.

I can also, for specific cash-rich clients, access renovated HMOs on long leases with all inclusive bills and management fees. This specific product needs to be bought for cash. My builder identifies certain geographically located properties for a specific price and then fully renovates them to order. Some clients need the security of a longer lease and 'guaranteed' cashflow to off-set their other financial commitments.

I will say it once again: if your service does not meet your client's needs, then you must find out and be clear about it. Refer them to someone else. Build referral relationships. The client may need to develop their personal financial strategy or mindset – give them a copy of one of my books!

Turning it on its head – the property comes first

Just to turn this on its head for a moment, I have been talking mostly about my model, which is based on my service. I also buy cashflowing properties in the north with the intention of holding on to them for the long term, during which time I will carry out one remortgage, at roughly the one-year stage, to release the bulk of my cash investment.

One of my business partners works the model the other way round and that is how we complement one another. They find deals in London for clients who are looking for potential capital growth. Then they offer the deal to their database, and then charge a percentage fee.

The difference is that I only look at property I intend to buy either for myself or a client, while they find deals and then offer them to a wider group, who may or may not be in a position to buy the deal at that time.

What do you want to become?

- An area specialist?

- A strategy specialist?

- A deal finder?

Or offer your working model?

Chapter 10

The contract and the paperwork

Think of your contract document as a 'process document' that explains to your clients exactly what you will do on their behalf and where their responsibility in the process starts and finishes. Don't consider it as a legal document to pursue someone in court; however, it should be detailed and may contain legal jargon.

Whether you buy a ready-made contract or create your own, I guarantee that you will redevelop it as your experience with clients increases. Initially, I only took payments on completion and then realised that clients could go part of the way through the process with me and then change their mind. I would not get paid for the research and time I had already spent!

I also recognised that in my sourcing business model, I was using contacts that I needed for my own portfolio development – they are really important to me. If a client pulled out after initially saying yes to a deal, that would damage my reputation and my relationship! I added in clauses that required stage payments for the work I was carrying out on behalf of clients. It also stated that if a client just 'changed' their mind, then there was a no-refund policy.

How you get paid – what you get paid for

Think through your process, understand the steps involved and the actions that you need your client to take. Write them down and maybe pass them to a friend to read through to check they make sense.

As you write down the stages of your buying process, think about what could go wrong at each stage, what it would have cost you to get to that stage and what you can do next. Let's think through a buying process:

1. As you carry out your research and search for a deal, there are costs such as travel and your time spent viewing the deals to be considered. Do you want to be paid for this? If so, how much? Now consider why the client would pay you for this – what are they paying for and what happens if you don't find anything?
2. So you have found a deal, how much information do you give the client straight away? Do they need to pay for this? If so, how much and why? What if they don't like the deal? What then?
3. They agree to buy – what now? I would assume that you might go ahead and negotiate a bit harder on the deal, maybe speak to a broker or solicitor. How much time will you spend? When will you be paid for this?
4. What happens if your client can't get a mortgage? What happens if the survey is bad or worse than expected?
5. How do you ensure that you get paid on completion?
6. What if it all goes wrong?

In a way, the development of your contract is like a risk analysis for your business. With a property deal you might consider the risk factors, the level of risk and everything you can do to mitigate those risks. The same is true with the client process; think through the steps, then consider what could go wrong, the level of risk of that happening and what the consequences (and costs) are to you. Lastly, think how you can mitigate the risks to an acceptable level.

For example, I used to give my clients the full postal code and access to all due diligence for a property upfront – in the days when I gave too much information, too much detail. One client asked to visit the property so that meant they had my agent details as well. This enabled them to go direct to my contact and cut me out of the deal. I did not get paid for two trips to view the property, my time negotiating the deal and arranging the visits and I had even incurred overnight expenses in a hotel. The issue being that I had not asked for any payment upfront. I may have been paid nothing but I did learn a valuable lesson.

If a client wants to view a property, I manage the process through my contract to ensure that I am fairly paid for research and contacts that I have made on a client's behalf.

Another client who did buy through me is now in direct contact with my agent to buy another property. Could I mitigate against this by putting in my contract that any future properties bought in the same area without my help would result in a £500 fee, or something to that effect? Would I put effort into enforcing it? I don't know! If a client does not recognise the value that you offer, that is a matter for their time and not your attention!

So now that you have a list of the stages of your business model, you will understand (as much as you can at this time) about what might go wrong and what you can do about it. You will even understand where your costs are in the process. This will give you your payment schedule. Whether or not you choose to ask for staged payments is entirely up to you and the level of your service. If you are just selling unqualified leads, then payment is full and final.

My model works for me, my lifestyle, my contacts, my knowledge and skill. You must be comfortable with the service that you are going to offer, especially if you are going to charge people money for it.

Making the deal secure

If you have spoken with your client, understood their needs and know that you can fulfil them, then you have a relationship. The contract lays out the terms and conditions, and also serves as another way of explaining exactly what you are going to do. As part of that explanation, you might ask for staged payments. As you present your contract to your client, you should have effectively secured your deal to the best of your ability. Remember, though, there is 'nowt as strange as folk'. Not everyone will share your business values or ethics.

Additional security comes in the form of your relationship with your estate agent, broker, solicitor and letting agent. If clients bypass you, it just means you did a good job. If they now want to use their own time travelling to the area, negotiating deals, then fine, you have plenty of other clients to work with – move on. You are busy doing it all again for another client or one of your existing clients who does value your time and the service you offer, someone who recognises that by leveraging your time they can spend their time doing other things.

What if it all goes wrong?

I suppose it depends on what you mean by 'all goes wrong'! To start with, you have written down your process, which means you understand what you are doing (to the best of your ability); you have considered the risks and looked to mitigate your expenses and protect your reputation through terms in the contract. If a client chooses not to buy or can't get a mortgage, then move on – you know the steps to take. Nothing is personal and challenges are just lessons spelt differently.

What *not* to do

Do nothing

If you do nothing, you will learn nothing – earn nothing – change nothing. Whatever you do, do it consciously – with purpose – and understand as many of the consequences as you can. Remember that as emotion goes up, intelligence goes down, and that is why you need to think and plan and do. Do something; whatever happens you will learn from it.

Make an offer you can't follow through on

This, for me, is fundamental. I only make an offer (in Scotland this would constitute a binding verbal contract) that I know – to the best of my ability – I can fulfil. Making an offer you can't follow through on lets down the vendor and the estate agent. Ultimately it will damage your reputation.

Panic or put your head in the sand

- If a client pulls out, find out why and resolve it.

- If a property falls through, find out why and resolve it.

- If an estate agent sells a property to someone else, find out why and refine the relationship.

Keep the estate agents, vendors, brokers, solicitors and builders informed as necessary. If you ignore a challenge or a problem, it will only get worse.

Doing it all again – moving on to the next level

At this stage, I thought I would combine 'doing it all again' with talking about moving on to the next level of business, as some of you will have already been sourcing deals and may not have thought of yourselves as running a business.

If you are already sourcing, then hopefully the last few sections will have taken you through a thought process that is already making you think about how you can develop your business. Now I want to talk about business growth.

There are two key factors in business growth: first, having the time to grow your business and, second, the systems in place to give you the time. Ironically, you may need the time to develop the systems that will then give you the time to grow your business!

Depending on your current position, you can pick and choose your way through the next few sections, but ultimately you will need to work through all of them if you want to increase your personal cashflow, grow your personal portfolio and eventually retire early.

Outsourcing

This does not have to be directly associated with your sourcing business. If you already own a property portfolio, this might mean employing a letting agent instead of self-managing, or handing over maintenance, refurbishments and repairs to another company. Now before you start arguing about how only you can do it and the cost of outsourcing, think back to Chapter 3, page 48 explaining time and ROTI. If you are still not convinced, then let's work through this exercise quickly.

I guarantee that whatever counter argument you come up with to justify why you don't need to outsource, I have already argued that myself. I effectively delayed the growth of my own business by at least a year if not 18 months. With hindsight, I can accept that it was for the right reason and it has worked perfectly for me, but at least acknowledge that you haven't yet outsourced because you are not ready (for whatever reason) and save yourself the constant merry-go-round. Either outsource or don't – the choice is yours – but you won't grow easily or as quickly without.

Where to start?

Record all your activities and how long they take you (I suggested this in Section 1) and then use your hourly rate to work out how much they cost you. I bet that you can buy (outsource) them for a cheaper hourly rate. Take, for example, my cleaner. She costs £10 per hour. I know that I can earn more than that in an hour. The trick to making outsourcing work for you is to actually work and earn money while the cleaner is doing the hoovering!

If you find the idea of outsourcing daunting, trust me I am right there with you. As I mentioned, it took me 18 months to actually outsource work successfully. I tried two friends and then finally went to a professional! In the space of a three-hour meeting, she understood what I did in a day, which tasks she could routinise for me and which tasks I could teach her to take over. We then identified the core essential activities that I had to do myself. Ultimately, almost everything I do can be routinised.

So once you have discovered your non-essential, non-urgent tasks (e.g. filing) and your essential, routine tasks (e.g. monitoring AST, gas certificates and rent), you can outsource them and then use that time to map out your systems with a view to creating a property administrator role. What things could someone carry out if they followed your precise instructions?

With your extra time and newly-discovered systems, you will have more time to do the bit that only you or your business partner can do, and really that is talking to clients. Everything else can be outsourced. As a part of my service, I guarantee my clients that I will view every property inside and out myself.

Maybe in future years I will choose to change that. Think about your service and what you are offering.

A brief word about systems

If you are an 'action taker', I imagine you will already be rushing to turn the pages – you don't want to think about, let alone read about, systems. BUT this is where money can be made. Not just in the sale of your systems, but more fundamentally in the development of your business.

By working through the systems you employ to find a deal, you can identify ways to improve and enhance your service and effectively increase your hourly rate. My original deal analysis spreadsheet was so detailed and complex that it took a week to enter and qualify the 12 deals that I had viewed in one day! I ran every scenario; I was double-checking and that was good in the early stages, but I actually took so long I lost some of the better deals because other investors put offers in before me!

The spreadsheet had beautifully coloured and designed boxes, each stage or option would print out perfectly. My spreadsheet now is a simple document containing only the key information of the primary strategy. I do not need a detailed analysis of every 'what if'; I just need to know that *if* 'what if' happens, I can work it out *if* needed! My new simple, black and white spreadsheet is completed in approximately an hour, depending on how many properties I have seen and how legible my handwritten notes are. I can then sort it, edit it and send it direct to my client.

Property management systems

The second area to consider is the property management system for your own portfolio. If you are using a letting agent, how do you monitor and manage the information flow on your current portfolio? Is stuff in your diary or in your head? Is it written down so someone else can do it for you or under your control because it is so important? 'Write it down', 'use a diary system' and 'use someone else' are actually the right answers to the questions above.

The 'need' to create space is what this section is all about. Without space you cannot grow your business.

Ideally, you need to spend your time building relationships with clients who you can sell property deals to. Could you focus on working with, say, six active clients at a time, which would mean finding one deal per week and completing roughly every six weeks? You could make £5,000 per working week, take eight weeks off a year for holidays, fun and personal development and still make in excess of £220,000 per annum. Less 40% tax (not counting expenses) would be £132,000 – is that enough? Is it worth giving your attention to systems and outsourcing?

Reputation and marketing

Once you have your systems in place and you have outsourced the non-essential tasks, you can focus on growing your business. How do you do this? Well, one easy way is to talk to more people – what if you could get people who were interested in property investment to come and find you, to want to speak to you and make themselves known to you?

This is where marketing comes in. I am not going to claim to be an expert marketeer – there are plenty of those out there. What I would rather do is, again, raise some questions for you to think about before you spend any money.

Who...? What...?

- Who is your client?
- What do they do now?
- What are they interested in?
- What are the problems that you can solve for them?

This is like marketing 101 – but maybe it is even more important to think about this now that we have a 'social media and global network'. There are so many dimensions in which we can communicate with one another – from the traditional 'just speaking to people' (but then you have to know which event to attend and who out of the 50–1,000 people to speak to) to a more massive media-enabled communication through websites and social media like Facebook, LinkedIn and Twitter.

If you are going to an event to speak to people one to one, then you can gauge their response to your words in real time through the expression on their faces. Even better, you can edit, revise and enhance what you have to say before you speak to person number two. Once you get involved in newspaper adverts, leaflets and the web you are not only committing yourself in 'print', but you are also committing yourself financially and it can be expensive to reprint leaflets or change websites.

You need to be clear about who you want to speak to and how they like to be communicated with. All of this might not be necessary if you are reselling bungalows to retired people. Get this clear before you start.

What is your offer? What makes you so special?

Now you know who you want to speak to, why would they want to listen? What makes you or what you have to offer so special? Why is your deal the perfect deal to solve all their problems? This is where the essence of you and what you are doing fits perfectly with your potential clients' values, wants and needs.

You need to do all the classic sales things like create your elevator or stadium pitch – your one-minute summary. You also need to get the tone and the language right – it's all about *them*, not *you*.

How can you prove it? Testimonials

What will your answer be if a client asks you: 'What have you done that earns you the right to talk to me?' Can you answer this question?

- Where were you before you started?

- What have you done?

- What have you got now?

- Who have you done it for?

- What did they think of your service?

Get some testimonials (note to self!). Get them in writing. Even better, get them on video too.

Now what I would say here is that, whatever your story, it is your story and it will be one of achievement. I don't think everyone has to be in debt to be successful – it's not a pre-requisite and it's not a competition. If you claim to be a wounded soldier, ex-junkie, alcoholic who was in debt by £100,000 and your partner left you homeless – cold on the streets – this does not automatically make you a good business partner or a success. Sadly, there are plenty of homeless people with similar stories.

The measure of success comes from the distance travelled and the amount of time you took to get there. Again, it is still not a race or a competition – it's about congruency and authenticity. Personally, I don't enjoy describing myself as a single parent, in social housing, unemployed with £100,000 on credit cards. That does not tell the story of who I was – even if some might think it makes a better 'story' for the tabloid drama that seems to attract people.

I was a single parent, former university lecturer who understood how money worked and played the credit card companies at their own game by manipulating 0% credit cards and high-rate savings accounts to my own advantage. I first went on a three-day property course in February 2008 and by the first bank holiday in May I had my area defined and I was connecting with estate agents, viewing properties and putting in offers for buy-to-let properties that I was going to fund with a cash pot created through a family joint venture partnership.

Sixteen months after my first completion, I was buying on average 1–2 properties per month for a year; I had a sourcing business and was just about to write my first book. I had enough personal cashflow that I didn't have to work. Tell your story your way, half full or half empty – it's all about the distance travelled and what you have learnt on the journey.

What do you like doing (speaking, writing or are you a 'background' person)?

This is back to knowing yourself and being in your flow. I know a number of property investors who are great with the numbers and doing the deals, but they are just not that fond of speaking to strangers or to groups. They do well because they have found people who they can partner with that complement them. Similarly, if you are all talk and no action or research, then you need a 'numbers and detail' person to make sure that things get done.

Other products

This is both a potential revenue stream and a form of marketing, but is it an area that you want to get into? I think the answer is yes. Over the years, I have worked with some great internet marketeers and website/online marketing geniuses. I think that the best thing I can say at this point is before you go online understand why you want to do it.

I regularly speak about 'making more money from your property knowledge' and in fact that is the underlying premise of this book… Start a sourcing business and leverage your knowledge and so make even more money from your property knowledge.

Well, once you have got to grips with running this model successfully, then you can start to think about other ways to make even more money from your property knowledge. Have you thought of packaging up your knowledge and experience in some form and selling it to other people?

There are lots of easy products that you can create to increase your exposure to your market, including e-books about key areas of your experience, websites/blogs and even videos. For example, what were you before you became a property business owner? Do you have transferable knowledge you could share? I know some good friends in property who offer a service to investors that saves them money on a refurbishment and can even reduce the purchase price. Could you do that? Could you write a book or hold a mini workshop?

Basically, everyone wants information – and a lot of people want to know how to make money, or rather more money. What do you know that can help people? You can think of your knowledge in two ways: as a free resource to your potential clients (investors or home sellers) that will help them and start to build trust so they come to you as their first point of call; or you can sell your knowledge as a product. Now I am going to be brief here because otherwise a small minority of you (having read a whole book about setting up a sourcing business and thinking it was a good idea) will get caught in the glare of the 'shiny' new idea (I have been there myself) and now be thinking about lots of online products – STOP!

The property sourcing business comes first – just bear in mind that, when the time is right, you can then repurpose your information and create lots of other products and services that can help your clients or create additional revenue streams. A word of warning – writing books seriously reduces your cashflow as you stop focusing on the number of deals you are doing!

Building the business with outside help – the challenge of the joint venture

I think that joint ventures are more of a challenge for two reasons: money and people. Either one is fine but put the two together and it becomes complicated because humans bring emotion and life with them.

If you change the thought of 'joint venture' into the concept of a 'property sourcing business', then the complications are largely removed. This is because you are either project managing the purchase of a property for someone in return for cash, which often equates to over three years rent share, or you can use their money to fund a deal – again for a fee. It is a business arrangement, which is also what a joint venture should be – it's just that some people forget to cover the detail of the agreement upfront!

Joint ventures need to be about business – a cold hard fact. What is going to be used/borrowed, for what purpose, for how long and at what cost? Then who will do what, where do the responsibilities lie? In a way, just like my sourcing contract, the joint venture document needs to explain the process that will happen to the money, which person has what role, time frames, consequences and ROI.

I prefer to think of joint ventures in a wider context of using other people's money; that way I am not limited to thinking about individuals or angel investors. Everyone is 'other people' so there are lots of sources of money – you just need to be clear on what you are going to do with it and how the owner of the cash will benefit financially.

I feel that this is an advance strategy because it takes us away from the simple repeatable sourcing business model. If you are working with someone who does not want to be an investor themselves, then the cash would be used for flipping or accelerated remortgages and that is a more risky strategy. It involves agreeing to borrow money (with penalties) for a set period in the hope that all things will stay the same while you renovate and refurbish a property in order to meet some predetermined valuation!?!

The point is that borrowing cash from individuals over relatively short periods of time based on future valuations is risky. Why not look more widely at other people's money and see how you can make it work for you? It may be on a slightly slower timescale – but certainly a safer one.

Chapter 11

So, to summarise the whole book…

If you have the mindset of a property business owner, understand how money works and run a replicable cashflow investment model, then it is just a matter of time before you have all the income you need.

In the sentence above the most important words are 'mindset of a property business owner' because, if you have that, then you are guaranteed to get the rest – you simply can't fail.

This book is all about the journey I have taken to become a property business owner, but it is not me or my journey that's important – it's what you recognise, feel and even know is relevant to you and what *you* want in life that is most important. In Chapter 1, I refer to 'active responsibility' as being my personal philosophy; in fact, it is the deciding factor in your success.

When you understand and apply 'active personal responsibility' to everything you do, then you will:

- be clear on what you want to achieve and 'constantly' monitor your performance against your goals

- understand how to leverage the relative value of money and identify massive ROI in every deal you do

- understand that when you face a challenge it is simply a lesson; you will have the skills to think logically about it, work out the message and then take appropriate action

- be aware of how you spend your time, and value and enjoy every moment because you are monitoring your actions against your goals – which are written down and shared with your mentor.

It sounds easy and really it is. What will determine how long it takes you to reach this state of business entrepreneurship is your level of resistance.

You might 'get' these concepts straight away; you might have to put more research or time into understanding the money markets, the maths or the practicalities of finding your area. However long it takes, you will be determined by your willingness to change your approach towards money and helping other people.

By now you will understand that by leveraging your financial resources first, you will be in a far better place to help those around you – it's the difference between thinking like a lottery winner and recognising that you need to put on your own mask first!

Remember that everything you have or do in your life now, is a result of decisions you have or have not taken in the past. Your decisions or lack of them are based on your values, the subconscious filters that you apply and the clarity of your focus. So, if you are happy with your life – fantastic – you did that; if you are dissatisfied in anyway whatsoever with your life, then you did that too. This is such an empowering thought – it means you have complete control over the outcome of your life. You can design it, build it, have it and live it. What you do today will change what you can do forever.

Remember, you have a choice – you can go down one of two paths: you can create a future life based on what you don't have in life right now – seeing only the gaps; or you can choose to create a life that is grateful for everything you have and focused on creating even more wealth, health and happiness. Which do you want?

'Who is going to support you?' is a question I haven't asked explicitly. I have talked about my coaches and the mentors that I read, observe or follow. I suggest that if you can see someone who has a life similar to your dream, then think about what values they might have, what they are focused on and what strategies they use. Why reinvent the wheel when standing on the shoulders of giants is much easier? Who is going to be your guide and hold you accountable to a higher level?

You are now able to:

- understand what you think and how past experiences have shaped you

- recognise the little voices that want to help, but might not be relevant anymore

- eliminate any limiting beliefs and adopt more empowering values and filters

- recognise the power of connecting with your whole mind

- take responsibility for your decisions and their outcomes, good or bad, noting the lessons and adjusting your course as you need to, to stay on the right path.

You are now able to master all the technical skills you need to apply to your business model by:

- identifying your personal point of financial equilibrium to get your income and expenses in balance

- calculating the value of your time and, therefore, knowing what strategies are worth your attention and which are a costly distraction

- leveraging your resources and using other people's money

- giving the lenders what they want and building a financial relationship on your own terms

- knowing what is important to watch in the world economy and making informed decisions about longer-term financial strategies.

So all that is left, of course, is to take action!

You are a business owner

You are taking this knowledge and understanding and applying it to your own circumstances. You are creating your own repeatable and replicable model of property sourcing. You have identified where your skills and experience lie and what your knowledge and passion are about. You know who you can go to for coaching, support and accountability.

You are following these steps to success, financial security and a fulfilling life:

1. Identifying **why** you want to invest in property, what you expect to get out of it, what the business will look like, how much you will earn (do the maths) and how you will earn your cashflow.
2. Getting financially **educated**; join us at our events.
3. Expanding your **network** by looking at who you mix with – what groups you attend or join. Again, come and hear me speak.
4. Choosing the right **strategy** in the knowledge that the other strategies can be used if necessary.
5. Remembering the value of your **time**! Understanding what you want to achieve financially and giving yourself the best possible chance of achieving it. Becoming your own client and making sure that you earn a decent income for your time.
6. **Leveraging** other people's money and other people's time. Understanding the relative cost of money and ROI and explaining the opportunity to potential clients.
7. Understanding what you have to **offer** your clients, what your service is and why they should buy from, sell or rent to you and not someone else.
8. Building the right **team** and mastering your leadership skills.

In Section 3, I explained, step by step, my replicable model of identifying and offering cashflowing properties to clients who have money or equity sitting in low returning vehicles and who want to make better use of their money.

I have created an online video course to take you through the whole process. I explain each step and then set you challenges and homework – you can find details on the website.

I know and really believe you can increase the money you earn from your property knowledge. I know you can build a better business. I also know that you will face challenges, otherwise you would not be reading this book. I am happy to support those of you who are serious about driving your business forward.

Whatever you do from now on is, of course, up to you – you are the creator of your future. Your life when you are 40, 50, 60, 70 and beyond is being created right now – what is your life going to be like? I'll see you scuba diving in the warm water coral reefs somewhere... ☺

Glossary

Asset: an investment that generates a profit – puts cash in your pocket.

AST (assured shorthold tenancy agreement): a contract between landlord and tenant explaining responsibilities and duties. Usually written for period of six months though can be longer.

B2L or buy-to-let: the process of buying a property with the intention of renting it to a third party to make a profit from the rent paid.

BMV (below market value): a specific term meaning a strategy that relies on getting a specific property valuation at a point in the future to enable all capital invested in a purchase to be recouped or released.

Bridging finance: a specific source of secured funding that some investors use to fund certain deals that require a quicker remortgage or are not eligible for mortgaging. This is an expensive source of funding and requires specialist advice.

EPC (energy performance certificate): legal requirement on any property being sold or rented.

ERC (early redemption charge): liable if you redeem a mortgage sooner than an agreed date.

HMO (house of multiple occupancy): often student housing or professional multi-lets. Each council will have their own area-specific requirements, but broadly any property over three storeys high with three or more unrelated occupants will be eligible for licensing.

Joint venture: usually refers to a business agreement to access someone else's cash for investment purposes – could be similar to a private form of bridging finance though often less expensive.

Lease option: a specific strategy aiming to control rather than own an asset or property. Popular in land and commercial deals – it has become popularised in the UK and like other more 'unusual' schemes it is under the watchful eye of the Financial Standards Authority. Eventually this will become a licensable strategy.

Leverage: the concept of taking a resource and multiplying the effect it can have – an example is buying a property using a mortgage where, for a fee, a lender supplies some of the capital required – another example is outsourcing where a person supplies time in return for a fee.

Liability: an investment or purchase that costs you money on a monthly basis – takes money from your pocket.

NMD (no money down): a strategy popular in 2008 to early 2010 where through various schemes 'deal makers' sought to offer properties for sale for a fee (to them) but no cash was actually required to purchase the house. The properties were then highly leveraged and often low or negative rent producing.

No money left in: a strategy that we all aspire to – the aim to buy a property and enhance its value so that at the point of remortgage you are able to release all the initial capital that you invested – leaving none of your own money in the deal.

ROI (return on investment): a useful tool to compare the benefit of investing in one specific asset compared to another, or compared to leaving funds in the bank.

ROTI (return on time invested): a tool to identify the real profit in a specific action, by including the cost of your time to ensure that a deal or purchase actually completes.

Strategy: this can be a way to describe the type of properties you buy, for example, buy-to-let usually means houses let on an AST or HMOs. It can also describe the type of investment strategy being used, for example, lease options, NMD or joint venture.

Yield: a figure to describe the average return possible based on gross figures.

Bibliography

Publications

Canfield, J. (et al) (2009) *Chicken Soup for the Entrepreneur's Soul*, Health Communications.

Dass, S. (2010) *Traders, Guns and Money: Knowns and Unknowns in the Dazzling World of Derivatives*, FT/Prentice Hall.

Evans, T. (2011) *The Art and Science of Light Bulb Moments*, O Books.

Hill, N. (1960) *Think and Grow Rich*, Highroads.

Kiyosaki, R. (2011) *An Unfair Advantage: The Power of Financial Education*, Plata Publishing.

Maxwell, J. C. (1998) *The 21 Irrefutable Laws of Leadership*, Thomas Nelson.

Metcalf, F. (2003) *Buddha in your Backpack*, Ulysses Press.

Morris, C. R. (2009) *Two Trillion Dollar Meltdown: Easy Money, High Rollers, and the Great Credit Crash*, PublicAffairs.

Olson, J. (2005) *The Slight Edge*, Momentum Media.

Rajan, R. G. (2011) *Fault Lines: How Hidden Fractures Still Threaten the World Economy*, Princeton University Press.

Robbins, T. (2017) *Unshakeable: Your Guide to Financial Freedom*, Simon & Schuster UK.

Rohn, J. (1993) *The Art of Exceptional Living* [Audiobook], Nightingale Conant.

Singer, B. (2008) *Little Voice Mastery*, Xcel Holdings.

Wusche, V. (2016) *Using Other People's Money: How to Invest in Property*, SRA Books.

Moving forward

Programmes, products and services

We believe that continuous professional development is critical for long-term business success. The world is simply moving too fast to stand still. Stop and you will be trampled.

We are continuously working with our clients through one-off strategy sessions or longer-term mentoring programmes to help them maximise their resources and make more money more easily.

You will find many free resources on my website, including a free newsletter focused on financial news, property investment and wealth creation.

Visit: www.vickiwusche.com/free-newsletter

Why train with us?

Do you want to invest in property for yourself or for others? Whatever your reason, we can help. Bringing over 11 years of property experience, combined with an education, business mentoring and coaching background, we are there to support you. From free resources, books, online and live courses to a full range of mentoring programmes – you will get direct access to Vicki Wusche, acknowledged by *The Telegraph* as one of the UK's top 25 most influential people in property.

Our ethos

You will have completely different resources and motives for investing in property than the next person. We treat you like the individual you are. We provide a range of teaching and learning materials from books and videos **for** private study, to courses and events. Our bespoke mentoring programmes are designed to support you in order for you to succeed in property.

Vicki Wusche leads all our training sessions personally, sharing her experience in property and business with a deep understanding of how we learn. Vicki will expand your knowledge whilst encouraging and supporting your vision, and hold you accountable to your goals.

We have designed four pathways to help everyone, no matter your personal objective, individual challenges or even preferred learning style. One of these pathways will suit you, whether you are new and curious and don't have a lot of money to invest, or whether you are interested but unsure, and even if you are a more experienced investor looking to move to the next level. There is something here to help you achieve your ambitions.

Drop us an email and we can help you find out the best next step in your business development.

Check the website www.vickiwusche.com

Vicki Wusche

Since 1994, Vicki has shared her knowledge and understanding of all things entrepreneurial, wealth and personal development. She has trained and spoken in front of thousands of people across the UK. In 2013, Vicki was recognised by *The Telegraph* as one of the UK's top 25 most influential people in property.

During her time working with the government to influence education policy and teaching across London, Vicki was privileged to inspire and educate entrepreneurs at the cutting edge of a new media revolution to build better businesses. At the same time, Vicki supported some of the most deprived people in London through her work as director for two charitable organisations that were focused on regeneration, housing, refugees, employment and inspiring young people.

During 2007, Vicki's attitude towards money changed dramatically. Having been made redundant in 2006, Vicki decided to step out as a full-time consultant. After working almost a year on a freelance basis, the challenges of self-employment led her to immerse herself in self-development. It was this, she now points out, that led to her success.

Vicki learned to recognise the power of leverage, the value of her time and how to maximise the return on her investments. Armed with this new understanding in 2008, she began to learn the mechanics of property investing, an interesting experience and one that initially seemed simple. However, challenge after challenge presented itself as she identified and 'tried' to buy investment properties. January 2009 saw a dramatic turning point as Vicki recognised she was either going to make a success of property investing or land a job stacking shelves!

Over the next 12 months she bought on average two properties per month and started her sourcing business. By 2010, Vicki's desire to share her knowledge and her understanding of property investing and using other people's money led her to publish her first book *Using Other People's Money: How to invest in property.*

Her ability as an author continued to develop and in March 2012 saw the launch of *Make More Money from Property: From investor thinking to a business mindset,* first edition. In August 2012, the second edition of *Using Other People's Money: How to invest in property* was published and, by November 2012, Vicki was launching her third book – *Property for the Next Generation: Preparing your family for a wealthy future* at the Business Show. By 2016, it was time for a fourth edition of *Using Other People's Money: How to invest in property,* replacing the 2014 update.

In 2015 Vicki decided to try something different and inspired by her mentor, Tom Evans, Vicki wrote her first fiction book – *The New Estate: Insights from the Twenty-Second Century.* This is a story of a world 85 years in the future that is radically different from ours. The narrator explains how we made the changes necessary for this new world to exist.

Throughout her employment and entrepreneurial endeavours, the driving forces behind Vicki are her family and her desire to help others maximise the resources they have, whether they be mental, emotional, financial or physical.

Combining all her skills and experience, and with an ability to passionately translate complex concepts into everyday practicalities, Vicki is focused on building property portfolios for clients who have access to financial resources.

Vicki's clients recognise that this is a once in a generation opportunity to build long-lasting financial security for their families and to secure and leverage their hard-earned wages before inflation erodes them. The clients, however, often lack the time to take advantage – that's where Vicki's experience and service comes into play.

In 2016, Vicki attracted a number of wealthy clients and in just six months she bought 14 properties, spending just under £1 million and generating an average of 10% net return for her clients. During the last seven years she has bought 63 properties and raised over £5 million in joint venture money.

In the last two years Vicki has expanded her mentoring and consultancy support beyond the property sphere. She works with a wide range of clients across all sectors by understanding the best use of their time and how to make more money more easily by selling through credibility.

Her clients range through a variety of SMEs from product based to the service industry, property related to pets, coaching to relocation. They all want the same result: business growth and financial security.

Together with her business partners, Vicki offers different levels of support for those looking to build their own business in property or expand their commercial businesses.

Why Vicki does what she does

When asked Vicki states:

I believe that I have stumbled on to something that can literally change your life.

Property investment has changed my life. I have moved from being a single mum living in social housing to owning a portfolio that provides decent homes for other families on benefits.

In the space of 10 years, I developed myself from being a benefit recipient to a property investor. From redundancy to business owner. From single mother to author and speaker. I recognised an opportunity to change my life and that of my children and I grabbed it with both hands.

My big vision is to change the way we think about property and community. To teach our children and families about money, debt, investment and opportunities. And to move from a materialistic world to one where people recognise when they have enough and contribute now, because they can help others. Where we value the young and the older members of society as they come together to share knowledge and experiences.

Why train with us?

Do you want to invest in property for yourself or for others? Whatever your reason, we can help. Bringing over 11 years of property experience, combined with an education, business mentoring and coaching background, we are there to support you. From free resources, books, online and live courses to a full range of mentoring programmes – you will get direct access to Vicki Wusche, acknowledged by *The Telegraph* as one of the UK's top 25 most influential people in property.

Our ethos

You will have completely different resources and motives for investing in property than the next person. We treat you like the individual you are. We provide a range of teaching and learning materials from books and videos for private study, to courses and events. Our bespoke mentoring programmes are designed to support you in order for you to succeed in property.

Vicki Wusche leads all our training sessions personally, sharing her experience in property and business with a deep understanding of how we learn. Vicki will expand your knowledge whilst encouraging and supporting your vision, and hold you accountable to your goals.

We have designed four pathways to help everyone, no matter your personal objective, individual challenges or even preferred learning style. One of these pathways will suit you, whether you are new and curious and don't have a lot of money to invest, or whether you are interested but unsure, and even if you are a more experienced investor looking to move to the next level. There is something here to help you achieve your ambitions.

Why do we create property portfolios for clients?

Property investment is something that can change your life for the better. We believe property is an accessible and controllable investment. One that can leverage the financial resources of a family in a safe, secure, and tangible way, to enable them to have more choice and control over their futures.

So, why invest with us?

We have been investing in property since 2004. We recognised just how significant a cashflowing property would be in preparing our financial security. So now we focus on generating cashflow for our clients. We work closely and individually with all our clients, to create, develop and implement your bespoke investment plan.

Our team will help you understand the different investment models, and to find the right properties for you. Whether you are looking for a hands- on style of investing with a larger cashflow from houses rented to multiple tenants (HMOs); or a more hands-free version with guaranteed rent, we will guide you through the maze of decisions. We also have development opportunities for investment or funding.

Most importantly, a strong team of experts are here to support the process. We view every property, manage any refurbishments or developments ourselves. We can recommend a team of professional advisors from brokers, to accountants, tax advice and inheritance planning.

Consider us your Personal Property Shopper – we look forward to working with you.

Check out Vicki Wusche's other products!

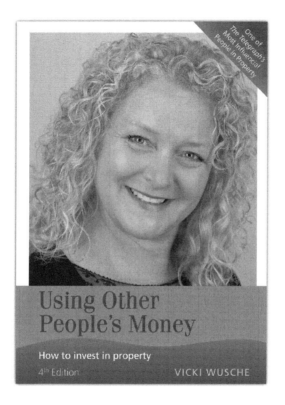

'This is a great read for someone like me just getting started in property investment and probably for other more experienced investors too. Vicki has grown her business from humble beginnings and more importantly started before the property crash and has survived to tell the tale. She has a wealth of experience and, probably more importantly, seems to be as passionate about helping other people as she is about her own property business. Thoroughly recommended.'

Mark (Amazon reviewer)

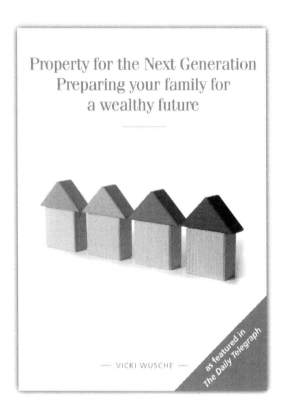

Property for the Next Generation
Preparing your family for
a wealthy future

VICKI WUSCHE

as featured in
The Daily Telegraph

'This is a very thought-provoking book and highlights some important issues that every parent should be considering. As someone whose second child is just buying their first house, I know the problems that can exist. If you want your children to be able to afford to buy a property, then read this book – whatever age your children are now. If you have ever thought property is "out of your reach", then this book will set you straight and help you get a leg on the ladder. Full of good advice with a no-nonsense approach.'

David J Millett (Amazon review)

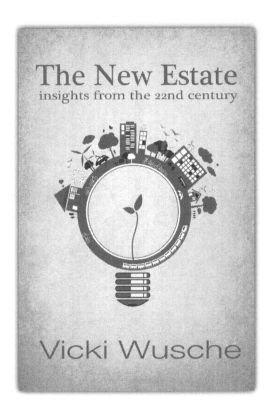

The New Estate
insights from the 22nd century

Vicki Wusche

'If you are interested in property, housing or life improvement theory then you must read this short and very thought-provoking book. Each paragraph invites you to challenge the author's thinking process around the idealism. It's like being teleported into the future where everything works out perfectly well whilst at the same time it feels like a revisit to the past when small businesses boomed and there was a strong community support structure. Skeptically is there "ever" enough time to make such a change, let alone 85 years? The key is everyone being on board with the idea of change and, of course, wanting the same results. How can this be? However, it is plain to see that dramatic change is needed in our housing systems and if it's imaginable, it's possible? Even though this book is written as a fantasy, if enough people can take just a few principles from Vicki Wusche's book, it's a big step in the right direction. Well worth a read over the weekend!'

Versatile Lift Company

'I thought I could use Excel and understood how to analyse a deal. This DVD really helped me understand what the numbers mean and I can now create and adapt my own spreadsheets. The other modules on the banks and the value of my time were useful too. A great buy, one I did not think I needed but I'm so glad I bought it!'

Comment received from a client after buying
the DVD at a property event

The Business Health Check

Do you really understand your property business?

- Identify essential business activities and prioritises you need to focus on
- Recognise the quickest route to make more money more easily
- Expose the gaps in your business plan and property strategy

To download the Business Health Check mini report, please go to:
bit.ly/BHC-Mini